Daily Devoti
FOR INDIVIDUAL

The Supernatural Power of a Transformed Mind

Access to a Life of Miracles

BILL JOHNSON

Unless otherwise indicated, quotations are from *The Supernatural Power of a Transformed Mind: Access to a Life of Miracles*, written by Bill Johnson and published by Destiny Image, and are marked with the corresponding page numbers from that book.

DESTINY IMAGE® PUBLISHERS, INC.
P.O. Box 310, Shippensburg, PA 17257-0310

"Speaking to the Purposes of God for this Generation and for the Generations to Come."

This book and all other Destiny Image, Revival Press, Mercy Place, Fresh Bread, Destiny Image Fiction, and Treasure House books are available at Christian bookstores and distributors worldwide.

For a U.S. bookstore nearest you, call 1-800-722-6774.
For more information on foreign distributors, call 717-532-3040.
Or reach us on the Internet: **www.destinyimage.com**

ISBN 10: 0-7684-2375-9
ISBN 13: 978-0-7684-2375-4

For Worldwide Distribution, Printed in the U.S.A.

3 4 5 6 7 8 9 10 11 / 09 08

Contents

Introduction

Revelation is not something you can dig out of a theological book or study guide. It's not even something you can unravel in the Bible all by yourself.

The Holy Spirit was sent to earth to be our own personal "study guide" through life. Jesus told us that *"when He, the Spirit of truth, has come, He will guide you into all truth"* (John 16:13). No book on earth, even the Bible, can substitute for our relationship with the Holy Spirit. My book, *The Supernatural Power of a Transformed Mind,* and this devotional and journal are designed to point more definitely to the fact that living the "normal Christian life" flows from a growing intimacy with Him.

With that in mind, I urge you to talk to the Holy Spirit each day before you use this devotional and journal. Invite His precious Presence to guide you into truth as you read and meditate. Have a journal where you can write down prayers and revelations that come from Him as you study. Ask Him to reveal Christ to you in greater measure. Ask for the grace and boldness to be not merely a hearer of His word, but a doer, that you might truly be wise and build your house upon Christ, the rock (see Matt. 7:24).

One of the primary purposes of *The Supernatural Power of a Transformed Mind* is to call believers back *up* to the wisdom of hearing and doing God's Word. There is an insidious and widely spread belief that knowing all *about* God constitutes true faith. To recognize this fallacy we have only to be reminded of James' admonition: *"You believe that there is one God. You do well. Even the demons believe—and tremble!"* (James 2:19). So be vigilant in your study to take a posture of willingness to hear and obey God.

Scripture tells us that seeking knowledge for its own sake only leaves us with fat heads (see 1 Cor. 8:1), among other things. This is not what will renew our minds. But the heart that seeks to please the Father and treasures the relationship with Him above all will not only receive revelation that renews the mind, but will pursue the purpose of that revelation and partner with God to see His will done.

The main principle behind the process of renewing our minds is that **we become like that which we behold.** We are not renewing our minds to have good thoughts; we are seeking to *see Him as He is* so we can become like Him. When we become like Him, we will do the things He is doing and say what He is saying.

Beholding Jesus is not intellectual; it is spiritual. It does not inform you; it transforms you. It is not an idea; it is an experience. It is not something you can have if you only read about it or study it. We can only behold Jesus by having a living encounter with Him. It is tragic that many believers understand that "sharing your testimony" of meeting Jesus merely means telling the story of how you got saved. Although that is glorious, our first meeting with Jesus was simply the doorway to a life of meeting Him, hearing His voice, feeling His love, and becoming like Him through the working of His indwelling Spirit. We can have a testimony every day of personally experiencing God's supernatural work in and around us.

My prayer for you is that by the end of this study, you will have as many testimonies of God's power and work in your life as the days it took to complete it, if not more. May Habakkuk's prayer be birthed in your heart: *"Lord, I have heard of Your fame; I stand in awe of Your deeds, O Lord. Renew them in our day, in our time make them known..."* (Hab. 3:2, NIV).

The Will of God:
On Earth as It Is in Heaven

OUR FATHER IN HEAVEN, HALLOWED BE
YOUR NAME. YOUR KINGDOM COME.
YOUR WILL BE DONE ON EARTH AS IT IS IN
HEAVEN.   (Matthew 6:9-10)

For most of my life I have heard people talk about seeking the will of God for their church, or their personal life, or their career. Many of us have treated the will of God as if it's unknown or unknowable.... But the will of God is simpler and plainer than we have thought.... The will of God is simply this: *"On earth as it is in heaven."* Isn't that basic? Isn't that refreshing? When we pray, *"Thy kingdom come, Thy will be done,"* we're praying for the King's dominion and will to be realized right here, right now.... God has not kept His desires secret: He wants the reality of Heaven to invade this rebel-torn world, to transform it, to bring it under His headship. What is free to operate in Heaven—joy, peace, wisdom, health, wholeness, and all the other good promises we read about in the Bible—should be free to operate here on this planet.... What is not free to operate there—sickness, disease, spiritual bondage, and sin—should not be free to operate here, period.

(Quote from *The Supernatural Power of a Transformed Mind:*
Access to a Life of Miracles, Page 32.)

Questions

1. The Lord's Prayer describes Heaven as the realm where the King's will is done. His nature and desires are perfectly expressed and fulfilled there. But on earth, God's will is not fully done. Read **John 1:12-13.**What other "wills" do you see here? Does the fact that other wills (besides God's) are at work explain why earth does not reflect His will?

2. If "*on earth as it is in heaven*" is the will of God, how do we recognize when Heaven is coming to earth? Much has been done over the centuries and called "God's will," but how do we know what God's will really looks like? Read **John 6:38.** Where did Jesus come from, and what did He come to do?

3. Jesus is the revelation of God's will. He showed us what Heaven (where the Father's will is perfectly expressed) looks like on earth. Look at a few Scriptures that support this: **John 14:9; Colossians 1:15,19; and Hebrews 1:1-3.** Since Jesus is the revelation of the Father, list some aspects of God's character that you see in Jesus.

4. **Acts 10:38** summarizes the ministry of Jesus, and **First John 3:8** echoes it. Read these verses and meditate on these questions:
   A. Why is it the Father's will to destroy the works of the devil?

   B. Why are those who sin oppressed by the devil?

   C. How did Jesus destroy the works of the devil? Besides breaking the curse of sin through His death on the cross, what specific things did He destroy as He ministered?

   D. With what was Christ anointed, according to Acts 10:38? Why did His ministry depend on these things?

Write down some of the "works of the devil" from which Jesus has freed you or others you know. Look for areas of breakthrough in your physical health, your emotional well-being, and spiritual torment or addiction. Thank God for bringing Heaven to earth in your life and in those around you, and pray the Lord's Prayer today for other areas where you need more freedom. Ask God for the revelation of His will to increase in your understanding.

Our Job: Proving the Will of God

A ND DO NOT BE CONFORMED TO THIS WORLD, BUT BE TRANSFORMED BY THE RENEWING OF YOUR MIND, THAT YOU MAY PROVE WHAT IS THAT GOOD AND ACCEPTABLE AND PERFECT WILL OF GOD. (Romans 12:2)

⋙ TODAY'S DEVOTION ⋘

Written into the DNA of every believer is an appetite for the impossible that cannot be ignored or wished away. The Holy Spirit, the very Spirit that raised Jesus from the dead, lives in us, making it impossible for us to be content with what we can only see, hear, touch, taste, and smell…. The normal Christian life begins with the realization that we were put here to do the will of God on earth as it is in Heaven—and what a joy it is to participate in that.

Has it ever occurred to you that one of your jobs on earth is…to prove the will of God? …Your calling and my calling as believers may be too massive to fully understand, but the Bible's command is clear: Our job is to demonstrate that the reality that exists in Heaven can be manifested right here, right now. We are not just to be people who *believe* the right things about God, but people who *put the will of God on display*, expressing it and causing others to realize, "Oh, so *that's* what God is like." … Jesus taught and demonstrated that the Kingdom of God is a present-tense reality—it exists now in the invisible realm and is superior to everything in the visible realm.

(Quote from *The Supernatural Power of a Transformed Mind:
Access to a Life of Miracles,* Pages 31, 35, 41.)

QUESTIONS

1. Read **Romans 8:14-17**. Who does the Spirit of God say that you are? How are you related to Christ and the Father?

2. Romans 12:2 tells us not to be conformed to this world. What—or who—are we supposed to be conformed to, according to **Romans 8:29**?

3. **Second Corinthians 3:18** gives us a clue about how the process of our conformation to the image of Christ occurs. This verse describes a present-tense, ongoing process. How do you suppose this process of beholding and being transformed differs from merely "believing the right things about God"? What is the Holy Spirit's role in this process?

4. In the previous day of the study you saw that Jesus' life and ministry revealed the Father's will and that He fulfilled that will through the anointing of the Holy Spirit. Today you are seeing that the Holy Spirit lives in you, conforming you to the image of Christ, and confirming that you also are a son or daughter of God called to reveal the will of the Father. Read the following verses in Matthew and consider these questions about your call to imitate Christ.

    A. Read **Matthew 4:17, 23**. How did the miracles Jesus performed "prove" His message was true?

    B. Read **Matthew 10:1,7-8**. How could and why did Jesus send His disciples out to do what He did as much as to say what He said? If He called His disciples to imitate and represent Him in deed as well as word, how can you expect Him to call you to anything less, now that you have His indwelling Spirit working to conform you to His image?

    C. Read **Acts 4:29-30** and **Acts 14:3**. Did you notice that the apostles linked their ability to preach with boldness to God stretching out His hand to heal and perform signs and wonders? Signs and wonders are God's witness, and as Scripture teaches, truth is established on the testimony of two witnesses (see Deut. 19:15; John 8:17). How do signs and wonders establish the truth of who God is—"prove His will"—when they accompany the teaching of the word?

Jesus' message was "Repent, for the Kingdom for heaven is at hand." The miracles He performed demonstrated the superiority of present-tense Kingdom reality over the works of the devil. Ask the Holy Spirit to give you deeper insight regarding the will of God that Christ "proved" and to help you follow in your Elder Brother's example. Thank Him for the present reality of the Kingdom within you (see Luke 17:21). Pray the apostles' prayer for boldness and ask for opportunities that require the Lord to confirm His word through demonstrations of power.

Submission to the Mission

ALL AUTHORITY HAS BEEN GIVEN TO ME IN HEAVEN AND ON EARTH.　(Matthew 28:18)

[**G**od's] idea was to have a planet engulfed in His glorious rule, with mankind flawlessly "proving the will of God" on earth as it is in Heaven.... Of course, we know the original plan got derailed, and that Adam forfeited the rulership God gave him over the earth, putting humanity into slavery to the enemy.... In the death and resurrection of Jesus Christ, God took back the authority man had given away and reclaimed our purpose on this earth.... We, the Church, are called to extend His rule in this earthly sphere, just as Adam was called to do....

But too few of us today follow those precise instructions.... Though well-intentioned, we become self-appointed in our commissions, honestly believing we are submitting to God. In reality, it isn't possible to prove the will of God on earth as it is in Heaven unless we are completely plugged into the primary mission God gave us.... First John 3:8 states clearly that through intimacy with God, we are to destroy the works of the devil.... That was Jesus' assignment; it was Adam and Eve's assignment; it was the disciples' assignment. Believers, *that is your assignment as well.*

(Quote from *The Supernatural Power of a Transformed Mind: Access to a Life of Miracles*, Pages 37-38.)

QUESTIONS

1. Today's study is going to look at the subject of commissioning in Scripture. Read **Luke 7:2-10**. The centurion said, *"For I also am a man under authority."* Whose authority was Jesus under? Why did the centurion understand that Jesus could do what He did because He was *under* authority? Why did Jesus call the centurion's response "faith"?

2. It's interesting that, according to the story, Jesus never met the centurion or his servant. But in a different way, they did meet. Read **Matthew 10:40**. How does this verse shed light on how delegated authority works?

3. Jesus often referred to Himself as One who had been "sent." Read **John 5:26-27, 30, 36**. According to John 5:36, what proves that Jesus was sent by God and operated under God's authority? You've seen that the works that Jesus did "proved the will of God," but how do they also prove that Jesus was operating under God's authority?

4. Just as Jesus claimed that He could do nothing in Himself, so you cannot hope to fulfill your commission to "prove the will of God" without being in complete submission to the Father as He was. Similarly, when you do submit to the Father, you should expect that He will give you "works" that bear witness to His authority. Read **John 14:12** and **Ephesians 2:10**.

   A. John 14:12 clearly links *believing* in Christ with doing His works, and here in this passage, as throughout the Book of John, Christ is specifically referring to the miraculous works that the Father gave Him to do as signs of His divine appointment. The promise that our faith would lead us to even greater works is huge! Why do you suppose believers have a hard time receiving this promise in faith?

   B. Do you think that the failure to believe what Jesus promises in these verses is the reason why many who would call themselves "Christians" don't get commissioned to fulfill the "primary mission" of destroying the works of the devil?

*If you have detected areas of unbelief in your heart, ask the Holy Spirit for help, as the man said to Jesus: "**Lord, I believe; help my unbelief**" (Mark 9:24). Invite Him to expose any area of your heart where you are trusting in something other than Him—our trust in other things is what keeps us from being fully submitted to Him. If He shows you anything, ask Him to guide you in transferring your trust and dependence to Him. If you desire, pray this prayer:*

"Jesus, I receive Your promise that, through faith in You, I would do greater works than You did in Your ministry. I believe You have sent the Holy Spirit to live in me and anoint me as He did You, that I might fulfill the works the Father has prepared for me. Help me to live in greater dependence on and greater obedience to You, Holy Spirit. I believe You want to send me into the world as You sent Jesus, so I will wait for You. I love You."

DAY 4

The Mind Is a Gatekeeper

...**B**UT BE TRANSFORMED BY THE RENEW-
ING OF YOUR MINDS... (Romans 12:2)

The only way to consistently do Kingdom works is to view reality from God's perspective. That's what the Bible means when it talks about renewing our minds....

The mind is actually a powerful instrument of the Spirit of God. He made it to be the gatekeeper of Kingdom activity on earth. The great tragedy when the mind goes astray is that God's freedom to establish His will on earth is limited. The mind is not to be tossed out; it is to be used for its original purpose. If the mind weren't vitally important to our walk with Christ and our commission, Paul wouldn't have urged us to "be transformed by the renewing of our minds." In fact, only a renewed mind can consistently bring Kingdom reality to earth.

....When we come into agreement with the primary mission, our minds become powerful tools in God's hands. This explains why there is such an intense war being waged for your mind and your mental agreement. Every thought and action in your life speaks of allegiance to God or to satan. Both are empowered by your agreement. Renewing your mind means learning to recognize what comes from hell, and what comes from Heaven, and agreeing with Heaven.

(Quote from *The Supernatural Power of a Transformed Mind: Access to a Life of Miracles,* Pages 42-44.)

QUESTIONS

1. What is "agreement"? Here's a little word study for you:
   A. In Hebrew, the root word for "agreement" is *chazah*, which means "to see."
   B. In Greek, the root word is *sugkatatithemai*, which means "to vote for."
   C. You could think of the "seeing" aspect of our agreement as the idea of "seeing eye-to-eye on something." Being in agreement means having the same perspective on a situation. You could think of the "voting" aspect in terms of "representation." When you vote for someone, you are saying that you are willing for them to represent you, and for you to represent or advocate for them.
   D. Consider these definitions of "agreement" in light of the fact that you are in "allegiance to God or to satan." The implication is that there are really only two candidates for your vote of trust, and they represent two opposite perspectives on reality.

2. How is agreement established? Well, if you think about it, a "perspective on reality" is a system of beliefs, a worldview. A worldview isn't so much *what* you see, as it is a *way* of seeing. The way you see reality is what determines what you think and how you live. In fact, you can't properly be said to believe in something unless there are behaviors in your life that reveal your dependence on that way of seeing. So in truth, agreement in our lives is established through *obedience*. Read **Romans 6:16**. What kind of bond is created through obedience? Can you see that obedience empowers the person you obey? Why does obedience require trust in the person you're obeying?

3. Now, most who call themselves believers wouldn't think that obeying satan was even a consideration. But if you listen to his lies and let them define your reality, you are actually obeying him. *One of the biggest lies to overcome is that believing in something means only knowing about it or acknowledging its existence.* This lie keeps you blind to what you truly believe, which is what you trust in and obey, and makes you content to have the "correct doctrine, but not correct practice" (p. 30). If you believe that Jesus is who He says He is, then you will obey what He says—your faith will bear fruit in your actions. Read **Matthew 7:24-27**. Both the wise and the foolish man heard the word, but what distinguished them from each other? What part of the house structure represents faith, or lack of faith? Does this illustrate the power of your worldview, your "way of seeing" reality, and how it causes you to build your life? Why is faith without works "dead," according to James 2:17?

4. There is a corollary issue that derives from redefining "belief": Your experience solidifies in you the conviction that, for example, although Christ and the first-century Church may have walked in power, you don't. You can end up building a case based on your experience for why you don't do what Jesus did. Yet among the commands He gave His disciples to pass on to each succeeding generation of believers are, "*Heal the sick, cleanse the lepers, raise the dead, cast out demons*" (Matt. 10:8). This is why "we must redefine 'normal' Christianity so it lines up with God's idea of normal" (p. 31). Read **Second Corinthians 5:17.**

A. What do you think it means to be a "new creation"? Do you think it at least includes the potential to experience things you've never even thought of before? Do things you've never done? What does it take to move past an attitude that says, "Anything can happen," to the attitude that says, "Impossible things *must* take place in order for me to walk as a new creation"?

B. Why do you suppose that people will admit that they experienced the super-natural power of God when they received salvation, but now, years later, they have no expectation to walk in the supernatural ministry of Christ? Do you recognize where "bad teaching and disappointment" have been contributing to that mind-set? Have you experienced unmet expectations in the area of encountering God?

JOURNAL/MEDITATION

*Take some time to talk out these issues with the Holy
Spirit. If you feel like you have "correct doctrine" without
"correct practice," ask the Holy Spirit to show you any
areas of un-renewed thinking into which you have slipped.
If you have stepped out in obedience and then stopped
when it didn't seem to bear fruit, ask the Lord if there is
fear or disappointment there. If He shows you anything,
confess it and ask the Lord to restore your hope and
expectation to walk into the "normal Christian life"
He's provided for you—a life filled with His supernatural,
life-giving Spirit and all the goodness that life brings.*

DAY 5

Repentance

R EPENT, FOR THE KINGDOM OF HEAVEN IS
AT HAND.   (Matthew 4:17)

Renewing the mind begins with repentance.... Jesus said, *"Repent, for the kingdom of heaven is at hand."* To many Christians, *repent* refers to having an altar call where people come forward and weep at the altar and get right with God. That is a legitimate expression of repentance, but it's not what the word repentance means. "Re" means to go back. "Pent" is like the penthouse, the top floor of a building. Repent, then, means to go back to God's perspective on reality. And in that perspective, there is a renewal, a reformation that affects our intellect, our emotions, and every part of our lives. Without repentance, we are locked into carnal ways of thinking. When the Bible speaks of carnality, it doesn't necessarily mean obvious, disgusting sin. Most Christians have no appetite for sin; they don't want to get drunk or sleep around, but because they live without the demonstrated power of the Gospel, many have lost their sense of purpose and gone back to sin. Having a renewed mind is often not an issue of whether or not someone is going to Heaven, but of how much of Heaven he or she wants in his or her life right now.

(Quote from *The Supernatural Power of a Transformed Mind: Access to a Life of Miracles*, Pages 44-45.)

1. Repentance, *metanoia*, literally means to change your mind. This doesn't just mean to think different thoughts, but to change what you believe about reality. What you believe is what determines the source of spiritual power you are drawing from and what sort of lifestyle that power promotes. As you learned in the previous study, there are two perspectives on reality that are vying for your agreement. Paul calls this distinction the difference between "carnal thinking" and spiritual thinking. Read **Romans 8:5-9**. Why do you suppose the flesh is opposed to the Spirit, rather than the "enemy" or the "demonic"?

2. Paul says that "to be carnally minded is death, but to be spiritually minded is life and peace." It's important to understand what Scripture means by "life" and "death." Read **John 8:51** and **17:3**. What particular aspects of death is Jesus saying you will not see if you keep His word? If "eternal life" is defined as "knowing God," then what does that say about the true nature of "death"? Does this understanding of life and death help you to recognize where they are presently at work in your life?

3. Read **Deuteronomy 30:15-20**.

    A. Is it a little unusual to think of life and death as things that you choose, rather than things that happen to you?

    B. Moses clearly defines the choice between life or death as a choice of the heart—to either love God and obey His voice or to turn away, become spiritually deaf, and serve other gods. Do you think this is a choice that you can make once, or often? Would it be fair to say that the battle over your mind is a battle of life and death?

    C. How significant do you feel that your daily choices to agree with God or obey your selfish desires are? Do you need to rethink that evaluation?

4. The purpose of God for your life keeps expanding as you move towards it and mature in your relationship with Him. That's why renewing your mind and producing "fruits of repentance" are things that will continue to go on throughout your life, as you daily choose life by agreeing with God. Read **Philippians 2:12-13**. You have been saved, but what process does Paul mention here that requires your lifelong participation? Who also is at work? What is the purpose of His work? Would you say the tone of Paul's admonition is one of awe over the reality that God is at work in and through you? Do you think this is the awe that is proper to have in light of the fact that you get to participate in "how much of Heaven [you want] in [your] life right now"?

JOURNAL / MEDITATION

*Repentance begins in the heart, because choosing life
is a heart choice to love God with all you are. A heart
that seeks to love God is a heart that can come to know
who He is, which brings a mind change that will enable
you to see reality from His perspective. That choice is
what enables you to "cling to Him," as the Scripture
says; and increased dependence on His presence can only
result in His supernatural invasion into your circumstances.
Invite the Holy Spirit to show you what it means to
choose life today—to love God and walk in His ways
in all of your circumstances and relationships. If you
are facing situations with unresolved conflict or seeming
impossibilities, ask Him to show you His perspective.*

Spiritual Senses

"EYE HAS NOT SEEN, NOR EAR HEARD, NOR HAVE ENTERED INTO THE HEART OF MAN THE THINGS WHICH GOD HAS PREPARED FOR THOSE WHO LOVE HIM." BUT GOD HAS REVEALED THEM TO US THROUGH HIS SPIRIT. (1 Corinthians 2:9-10a)

Written into the spiritual DNA of every believer is an appetite for the impossible that cannot be ignored or wished away. The Holy Spirit, the very Spirit that raised Jesus from the dead, lives in us, making it impossible for us to be content with what we can only see, hear, touch, taste, and smell. Our hearts know there is much more to life than what we perceive with our senses; we are spiritually agitated by the lack of connection with the realm of the supernatural....

(Quote from *The Supernatural Power of a Transformed Mind: Access to a Life of Miracles*, Page 31.)

QUESTIONS

1. Start by reading the whole passage, which begins with the opening verse for today. Read **First Corinthians 2:9-16**. This passage explains that the things God has prepared for you cannot be perceived through your physical senses. How then do you perceive them, according to verse 10?

2. Verse 14 says that spiritual realities are spiritually *discerned*. "Discern" means "to examine or judge." The next verse says that the spiritual person "judges all things," and the reason given is, "We have the mind of Christ." Therefore, discernment, the faculty by which you perceive spiritual realities, is a faculty of the *mind*. Your mind's ability to perceive is directly related to the spiritual source you are setting your mind on—that with which you are *agreeing*. Describe the connection between the Spirit and your mind in these verses: **Ephesians 4:23** and **Second Timothy 1:7**. Now, what is the Holy Spirit helping us to discern, according to **John 16:13-15**? Would you say that it's a pretty awesome job the Holy Spirit has, to take "all things" that belong to Jesus and the Father and declare them to you? Do you believe that the Holy Spirit is speaking to you continually? Does this explain why "our hearts know there is much more to life than what we perceive with our senses"?

3. Let's look at another job of the Holy Spirit. Read **Romans 8:26-27**.

    A. Can you see the Holy Spirit in these verses as your go-between, telling you what Jesus is saying, and then telling the Father what you need, even when you can't put words to it? How does that make you feel?

    B. This verse says He makes intercession for us according to what? Given the understanding of the will of God to be "on earth as it is in heaven," what do you suppose is on the Holy Spirit's heart for your life?

JOURNAL/MEDITATION

*The Holy Spirit in you has given you all the equipment you need to perceive spiritual reality, and He has lots to show and tell you about Heaven! Jesus promised that He would guide you into **all truth**. Take some time today to thank the Holy Spirit for His presence in your life. In your prayer time try talking less, and ask the Holy Spirit to speak to you or show you something about who He is and how He feels about you.*

Seeing the Unseen

WHILE WE DO NOT LOOK AT THE THINGS WHICH ARE SEEN, BUT AT THE THINGS WHICH ARE NOT SEEN. FOR THE THINGS WHICH ARE SEEN ARE TEMPORARY, BUT THE THINGS WHICH ARE NOT SEEN ARE ETERNAL.

(2 Corinthians 4:18)

Jesus taught and demonstrated that the Kingdom of God is a present-tense reality—it exists now in the invisible realm and is superior to everything in the visible realm....

To be of any use to the Kingdom, our minds must be transformed. We find a clue to what that word means in the transfiguration of Jesus when He talked with Moses and Elijah. The reality of Heaven radiated through Jesus, and He shone with incredible brilliance. His body revealed the reality of another world. The word *transformed* in that passage is the same word we find in Romans 12:2. The renewed mind, then, reflects the reality of another world in the same way Jesus shone with Heaven's brilliance. It's not just that our thoughts are different, but that our way of thinking is transformed because we think from a different reality—from Heaven toward earth.

(Quote from *The Supernatural Power of a Transformed Mind: Access to a Life of Miracles,* Pages 41-42.)

QUESTIONS

1. The above verse from Second Corinthians describes the distinction between the invisible and visible realms in terms of *time*. The invisible reality is eternal, while the visible realm is temporary. Bible teacher Jack Taylor says, "The measure of reality is permanence." That means that the things that are more enduring are more *real*. This is why the invisible, heavenly reality is a *superior* reality. Take a look at some things Scripture says about heavenly reality. Read **Mark 16:19**. Where are you and all the saints presently and in eternity?

2. Read **Colossians 3:1-4**. Where are you to set your mind? Why do you suppose you have to make a conscious effort to focus on eternal reality, where you already are, more than your temporal circumstances?

3. Now look again at **Second Corinthians 3:18**. Does this verse describe the process involved in your "reflecting the reality of another world"?

   A. What does it mean to "behold" Christ? What aspects of your spiritual senses are involved in that process?

   B. "Beholding," "setting your mind," and "being transformed" are meant to be ongoing in your life. What sort of practices and disciplines do you have and/or need to cultivate in order to sustain a deeper focus, not just on thinking about Christ, but on entertaining His presence by His Spirit?

4. **Hebrews 11:1** and **11:6** offer some final thoughts on what it means to perceive and reflect heavenly reality. What is the "evidence" of unseen reality? How does faith "reflect the reality of another world"? What two things must qualify your belief in the nature of God in order to please Him?

Do you really believe that God rewards those who diligently seek Him? How does that play out in your daily choices to pursue God? Take some time to write down the "evidence" of God's rewards in your life as you have sought Him. Thank Him for being true to Himself and to you in your relationship. Ask the Holy Spirit to unfold in your understanding and experience the process of setting your mind on things above and beholding the glory of the Lord with an unveiled face. Write down what you hear and see!

Seeing the Kingdom

JESUS ANSWERED AND SAID TO HIM, "MOST ASSUREDLY, I SAY TO YOU, UNLESS ONE IS BORN AGAIN, HE CANNOT SEE THE KINGDOM OF GOD." (John 3:3)

Most Christians have repented enough to be forgiven, but not enough to see the Kingdom. They go part of the way, then stop. Did you know that meeting Jesus was only the first step in your Christian walk? Conversion puts you at the entrance of an entirely new way of living, but there is a lifetime of experiences beyond the entrance that many folks don't experience. They never enter into their full purpose. They spend their life rejoicing just on the other side of the river shore, but never move in to take the cities and inhabit the promised land. It's not enough to barely make it across the river into the promised land; we must go all the way and fight for the territory God has promised to His Church. Life is so much fun when we experience the miraculous and partner with the supernatural! It's an honor and privilege and responsibility that too many of us have feared and ignored.

The idea of Kingdom power and spiritual conflict unsettles some people, but without power, the Gospel is not good news.

(Quote from *The Supernatural Power of a Transformed Mind: Access to a Life of Miracles*, Page 46.)

QUESTIONS

1. The Promised Land is a prophetic picture of the life that God desires for you to live, a life where His "great and precious promises" are fulfilled in your life. The Bible is filled with promises that are beyond your ability to comprehend. But there are certain "pillar truths" about the nature of God that, once they are established in your way of thinking, will make these promises seem an indispensable part of being in a covenant relationship with the God of the Universe. One pillar truth is found in **Luke 1:37.**

    A. The literal translation of this verse is, "For with God no spoken word [*rhema*] is without ability." That means, when God speaks His promise to you, it comes with power to accomplish what was said. Think about that for a minute. Could the implication be that every time God speaks to you, it is proper to respond as Mary did in this context: "Let it be to me according to Your word"?

    B. When you have read promises in Scripture, heard the Holy Spirit speak them to you, or received prophetic words over your life, has it been easy to respond like Mary? If not, do you think part of the problem lies in the fact that you are more focused on your lack of ability than the ability of God's word?

2. Now take a look at the mind-blowing promises in **Romans 8:31-32.** Consider Paul's questions for a moment. They are rhetorical, but if the answers are obvious, they are also absolutely stunning and, honestly, probably foreign to the way many believers still think. Do you really believe that God will freely give you *all things*? How important is it for you to believe this if you are going to walk in the supernatural ministry of Jesus?

3. You've already looked at Jesus' promise that those who believe would do greater works than His. The next two verses are equally awesome to believe. Read **John 14:12-14.** Isn't this a confirmation of the promise you saw in Romans? What key does this verse provide for you to enter into the promise of receiving "all things" from the Lord? Do you regularly ask Jesus for the things you need to fulfill His purposes in your life?

4. Now read **First John 5:14-15.** This shows how John himself believed Jesus' promise, and how you can respond to it as well. You are supposed to ask according to *what*? If that qualifier has made you unsure about what to pray for in the past, remember that the will of God is *"on earth as it is in heaven."* How does that definition free you to ask "according to His will"?

JOURNAL/MEDITATION

Take some time to look over or write down a list of the key prophetic words and promises that the Lord has given you over the last year or two. If there are some that look impossible in your current circumstances, thank God for them! It's usually the very things we can't do of ourselves that God is calling us to do so that He will be glorified and shown strong in our weaknesses.

Thank Him for His ability to fulfill His Word, and pray Mary's prayer over your words. Then take some time to imagine what needs to take place for you to enter into the fullness of the promises, and ask the Holy Spirit to give you insight into this. Make a list of resources you need physically, emotionally, spiritually, and materially in order to fulfill the revealed will of God for you. Go through the list and ask God for each thing that you need, thanking Him for hearing you and declaring His faithfulness to fulfill His Word in your life.

Called to the Impossible

THEN JESUS ANSWERED AND SAID TO THEM, "MOST ASSUREDLY I SAY TO YOU, THE SON CAN DO NOTHING OF HIMSELF, BUT WHAT HE SEES THE FATHER DO; FOR WHATEVER HE DOES, THE SON ALSO DOES IN LIKE MANNER."

(John 5:19)

Many believers think miracles and power are for extra-special anointed people of God. Many get hung up on the idea that Jesus did miracles as God, not man. In reality....He did miracles as a man in right relationship with God because He was setting forth a model for us, something for us to follow. If He did miracles as God, we would all be extremely impressed, but we would have no compulsion to emulate Him. But when we see that God has commissioned us to do what Jesus did—and more—then we realize that He put self-imposed restrictions on Himself to show us we could do it too. Jesus so emptied Himself that He was incapable of doing what was required of Him by the Father—without the Father's help. That is the nature of our call—it requires more than we are capable of. When we stick to doing only the stuff we can do, we are not involved in the call.

(Quote from *The Supernatural Power of a Transformed Mind: Access to a Life of Miracles*, Pages 48-50.)

QUESTIONS

1. One of the most difficult tendencies to correct in an American Christian is self-reliance, because most Americans grow up believing that maturity looks like being completely self-sufficient. Jesus demonstrated the complete opposite—His maturity grew as He grew in dependence on His Father. Read **Matthew 4:1-2**. One of the reasons you are called to practice the discipline of fasting is that it teaches you to be dependent in a way you would probably never choose for yourself. Have you ever had your heart tested by having to wait to eat and enduring hunger? If God told you that you were going to be tempted by the devil himself in 40 days, would your first instinct be to put yourself in that state, empty of physical strength?

2. The apostle Paul learned how to make room for the power of God to be demonstrated so the faith of new converts would be in God, not in his gift. Throughout his Epistles it becomes apparent that Paul discovered Christ's secret to walking in power—emptying Himself and becoming totally dependent on God to fill Him. Read **Second Corinthians 12:9-10**. Think about the last time you felt insecure about a relationship, or physically tired, or overwhelmed by a task facing you. Was it natural to rejoice in your weakness? How can we train your heart and mind to run to the Lord instead of fixating on your lack?

3. Many Christians feel weak when they are confronted with the commission to walk in the miraculous ministry of Christ. But in the previous verse, the grace that was sufficient for Paul was not just for enduring difficulty, it was to enable him to fulfill his commission, no matter what the circumstance. He explains this in **Second Corinthians 3:5-6**. What did the Lord make Paul? Won't the Lord do the same for you?

4. Your ability to say "I am strong" in the midst of your weakness comes from precisely that which Paul was so zealous to establish in the Corinthians—*faith in God's power*. Among the list of faith-exploits of the heroes of faith listed in Hebrews 11 is the phrase, *"out of weakness* [they] *were made strong"* (Heb. 11:34). But more than believing that God was *able* to do what they could not, these men and women had a revelation that it was the Father's *nature* to perform the impossible through people of faith. Read **Hebrews 11:11** and **Second Timothy 1:12**. Why does God's faithfulness require Him to demonstrate His power in your life? Can you see that having faith has more to do with trusting our lives to Someone than exerting some kind of mental effort to have faith in individual truths and principles for our circumstances? Does it follow that the measure of faith you're walking in is directly related to your depth of intimacy with God?

You apprehend the promises of Scripture for your own life by strengthening your belief that the same God who was with all the heroes of faith and Jesus Himself is with you and in you by the Holy Spirit. Your trust grows as you depend on Him to come through in impossible situations. That is where you gain the personal revelation of His faithfulness to be Himself in your life. And each time He proves Himself, you have a witness to declare to those around you, "This is who God is!"

Take some time today to recount your history with God. Take one or two breakthroughs you've experienced and meditate on what particular aspects of the nature of God were revealed to you in those experiences. Or you may be facing a new obstacle and there is a hero of faith whose story prophesies that God has precisely what you need. Ask the Holy Spirit to show you a figure in the Bible or in history who faced a similar obstacle and saw God reveal Himself as the answer. Declare Him to be the same in your life today and in the future.

The House of God: His Dwelling Place

T HEN JACOB AWOKE FROM HIS SLEEP AND
SAID, "SURELY THE LORD IS IN THIS PLACE,
AND I DID NOT KNOW IT…. THIS IS NONE
OTHER THAN THE HOUSE OF GOD…."

(Genesis 28:16)

✦ TODAY'S DEVOTION ✦

The Bible talks a lot about our being a dwelling place for God, and "God's house" on earth. What does it mean to be "God's house"? ...Because [Genesis 28] is the first mention in the Bible of the House of God, this passage defines the nature of the subject for the rest of Scripture. There are several aspects of this house that we should pay attention to. First, Jacob said, "God is here and I didn't even know it." This tells us that it is possible to be in the presence of the "House of God"... and never know it's there. In other words, without a revelation—in Jacob's case, a dream—we can be oblivious to the presence and work of God in our lives or around us.

The other important thing about the House of God was that it functioned under an open Heaven, meaning the demonic realm was broken off and there was clarity between the realm of God's dominion and what was happening on earth. It was pictured in Jacob's dream as a ladder with angels ascending and descending....

The fulfillment of the House of God began with Jesus. He was the House of God on earth. But this concept did not stop with Him—far from it. He was the initial fulfillment of the House of God, but not the ultimate fulfillment.... We, the Church, the redeemed, are the tabernacle of the Holy Spirit, the eternal dwelling place of God! We are living stones, according to First Peter 2:4-5, fitly framed together, building the eternal dwelling place of God. The House of God is us! Jacob's dream was not just about the Messiah but about you and me and every born-again believer throughout history. It is the heart of our very identity.

(Quote from *The Supernatural Power of a Transformed Mind: Access to a Life of Miracles*, Pages 55-58.)

QUESTIONS

1. There are many examples in Scripture of people interacting with God while being unaware that it was God with whom they were dealing. Look at a classic example in **Luke 24:13-16**. What do you think it means in verse 16, that "their eyes were restrained"? The language suggests that this was something that was happening *to* them, not something they were doing. Why do you suppose Jesus would keep His identity hidden from them?

2. Continue reading on in the story: **Luke 24:17-32**. In verse 31, once again, the disciples' revelation is a matter of something happening to them rather than something they are doing. Why do you suppose Jesus would choose to reveal Himself, but only for a moment? Do you have moments of revelation like this, where suddenly you see what the Lord has been doing all along in your life? Are you able to recognize symptoms of His presence, as the disciples did when they said their hearts burned as they walked with Jesus? Has it helped you become more aware of His presence on a daily basis? What value do you have for those moments of revelation, and what do you think the Lord's purpose is in opening your eyes? Do you pray for revelation like this often?

3. Since Jesus is the fulfillment of the house of God, then the elements of the House of God can be seen in His life and ministry. Look at the evidence of the open Heaven over His life. Read **Matthew 4:24** and **Matthew 12:28**. How does Jesus' ministry show us what an open Heaven looks like, where "the demonic realm [is] broken off and there [is] clarity between the realm of God's dominion and what [is] happening on earth"? Does Jesus' act of displacing the rule of demons by the rule of the kingdom reveal the presence of an open Heaven over Him? What does that suggest about the relationship between an open Heaven and the manifestation of the Kingdom?

4. What are the implications of the statement that "there is an open Heaven over each one of us, from the newest Christian to the most mature" (p. 59)? Read **Luke 17:20-21**. What does it mean that the Kingdom is within you? How does your life demonstrate "clarity between the realm of God's dominion and what [is] happening on earth"? How has the demonic realm been displaced in your life? Can you recognize that the departure of the demonic was caused by the coming of the Holy Spirit to dwell in your life? Why is your identity as the dwelling place of God the essential foundation for your commission to carry on the supernatural ministry of Christ?

Think about a time when you had a revelation of what God had been doing in your life—maybe in little things you initially thought were just coincidences or bright spots in your day. Pay attention to the specific pieces of the trail of evidence that He unveiled to you. What were the manifestations of His presence in your life, like the "burning hearts" of the disciples? Do you recognize any of those things going on in your immediate experience? Ask God to unveil Himself to you again today and deepen your awareness of His continued ministry to you and through you by His Holy Spirit.

The House of God: The Gate of Heaven

... **O**N THIS ROCK I WILL BUILD MY CHURCH, AND THE GATES OF HADES SHALL NOT PREVAIL AGAINST IT.   (Matthew 16:18)

Being the House of God means we have the exact authority Jesus has at the right hand of the Father. We are entitled and empowered to be His "House," His embodiment on earth. As a Christian at this very moment, you have absolute liberty and access to Heaven....

You'll remember that Jacob said, *"This is none other than the house of God, and this is the gate of heaven!"* ...In this context and elsewhere in the Bible, "gate" seems to mean a place of transition and access.... When we talk about the Church being the gate of heaven, we are referring to the place where the reality of His dominion becomes available for all of mankind—His world invades ours! ...Has it ever occurred to you that we're on offense, not defense? The principalities and powers that set up dominions or "gates" all over the earth will not prevail against *us*! We are advancing and winning, and Jesus promises that in the end, no gate of hell will stand. Wow!

So where precisely are the gates of hell? ...You'll recall from our discussion of renewing the mind that I called the mind the gatekeeper of the Kingdom of God. It is the place of access, transition, and power. It follows that the gates of hell are set up in people's minds.... A most important thing to remember is that the devil is empowered by human agreement! ...To say, "I'm only human," is to say, "I'm only satanic." Humanity without Christ at the center is satanic in nature. When you've been given the Spirit of God, you lose the privilege of claiming, "I'm only human." You are much more than that!

(Quote from *The Supernatural Power of a Transformed Mind: Access to a Life of Miracles*, Pages 59-61.)

QUESTIONS

1. Start by reading the full account of Jesus' statement about "building His church" in Matthew **16:13-18**. Most commentaries explain that the "rock" on which Jesus would build His church is the confession of faith in His true identity as the Son of God, like the confession Peter makes here. But what precedes the confession is, as Jesus explains, the *revelation* of that truth, which is something only God can give.

    A. Why does your knowledge of Jesus' true identity only come by revelation from God? What is the difference between hearing *about* who Jesus is and having a revelation of who He is?

    B. Can you see that a confession that *agrees* with the Father's revelation to you of Jesus' identity is an act of faith? Remember, faith is agreement that empowers the reality of what you believe to manifest in your life. The reality of God's kingdom is released and established through the faith of His people.

2. Now look at **Second Corinthians 10:3-6**. In Matthew 16, Jesus is describing the military advance of His Church against the gates of Hades. These verses in Second Corinthians are describing some of what that advance looks like. What exactly are the enemies that you are casting down and bringing into captivity? Where do you suppose this battle is taking place? How does this support the author's locating the gates of Hades in the mind?

3. Perhaps when you compare your life to the way Jesus lived, you notice a distinct gap between His quality of relationship with His Father, His purity, and His power, and those you presently experience. But the reality that you have the same access to Heaven that Jesus did, that you walk under an open heaven, and that you are no longer "mere men" is not based on your experience. Failure to consistently seek experience in what God says is true about you is what can allow arguments, imaginations, and thoughts to exalt themselves above the knowledge of Christ and bring the enemy's influence into your life. But Jesus said that the revelation of who He is, and your confession of faith in that revelation, would be strong enough to push back those hellish points of access in your mind. This passage in Second Corinthians gives some keys for how to put that revelation and confession to work in your battle against hell.

    A. The first aspect of your battle is "casting down arguments and every high thing that exalts itself against the knowledge of God." As you grow in your understanding of the truth through your relationship with the Holy Spirit and knowledge of Scripture, it will become easier to recognize the things that are seeking to exalt themselves against the knowledge of God. But how do you *cast them down*? How do you keep the knowledge of God in a high place?

These things are vital to discover. How is this different from arguing with people about what is true? How would you describe the part that our mind—as the "gate of Heaven," releasing heavenly reality against the gates of Hades—plays in this?

B. The second aspect of your battle is "*bringing every thought into captivity to the obedience of Christ*." How do you take a thought captive? Have you noticed that thoughts and arguments that are exalting themselves above the knowledge of God work to take you captive—or "captivate" your attention? How does your focus on heavenly reality—that which you are seeking to release here on earth—enable you to bring thoughts into submission to Christ?

Remember, **obedience** *is the thing that establishes our agreement with a particular perspective on reality—either God's or the enemy's. Let's say that you have a bill due and don't have the money to pay it. There are two different perspectives on your situation. If you focus on your lack of money and start worrying, thinking incessantly about how you can possibly fix your problem, it's not too long before you're overwhelmed and hopeless. You probably start turning to other comforts to ease your sense of burden. But if you focus on God's promises to you and the testimony of His faithfulness in your past, you rest in peace, knowing that the provision or the key to access it will be provided. You receive comfort from the Comforter Himself.*

Your response is an act of obedience in both cases to one or the other perspectives, and those perspectives are speaking to your mind at all times. Can you see how taking each thought captive and making it **obey** *Christ is really the battle we all have in maintaining our focus on God's perspective? The lies that the enemy sends us to get us to start seeing our circumstances from a different perspective are working to dislodge our focus on the truth. When we lose our focus, our faith—which is drawing the reality of Heaven into our lives through agreement with the truth—falters. Do you recognize this battle for your focus? How do you fight to keep your focus on God's perspective?*

DAY 12

Binding and Loosing

$$A^{\text{ND I WILL GIVE YOU THE KEYS OF THE}}$$ KINGDOM OF HEAVEN; AND WHATEVER YOU BIND ON EARTH SHALL HAVE BEEN BOUND IN HEAVEN, AND WHATEVER YOU LOOSE ON EARTH SHALL HAVE BEEN LOOSED IN HEAVEN.

(Matthew 16:19, NASB)

This was the entire focus of Jesus' ministry, and it's a great word of authority to us. Whatever we bind has already been bound. Our task is to see what is bound up there, and then bind it down here. Whatever is free in the heavenly realm to function needs to be released here. We are to be a gateway people for the free flow of heavenly realities into this planet.

How do we know what is bound and loosed in Heaven? Who tells us what Heaven's reality looks like? The only way to know these things and to function as the House of God and gate of Heaven is to have revelation of what is happening in Heaven. Otherwise, we're working in the dark. God has always wanted to release truth to His people, backed by the Word, of things that are found in Heaven but have no earthly parallel.

(Quote from *The Supernatural Power of a Transformed Mind:
Access to a Life of Miracles*, Pages 62-64.)

QUESTIONS

1. What does it mean that you've been given the keys of the Kingdom? Look at two Scriptures that mention keys: **Isaiah 22:22** and **Revelation 3:7**. These verses provide the foundation for Jesus' promise to give us keys—He has them to give us because He received the key of David, the symbol of God's chosen authority. Keys are a symbol of authority because a person with keys has *access* to places that other people don't, as well as the power to *shut* places of access. So when Jesus promises you keys, He is promising you access. What do you think it means that you have access to the Kingdom? Do you think this includes access to all the realms of God in Heaven? What sort of "rooms" in Heaven do you suppose these keys will open? Doesn't access to the "doors" imply access to what's behind them?

2. The next part of the verse talks about binding and loosing. In order to define those terms a little, look at a passage in which Jesus used the word "bind" to describe what He was doing when He delivered people from demonic torment. Look at **Matthew 12:29**. Since binding a strong man requires us to be stronger than the strong man, does it seem here that "binding" has to do with power? Jesus gave His disciples power over all the power of the enemy in Luke 10:19, but how do you know how to access and use that power?

3. You need authority, not just power, to operate in binding and loosing. Jesus connects binding and loosing with keys, the symbol of authority. They are primarily *legal* terms. Remember, the context of this verse in Matthew is the revelation of Jesus' identity and the foundation of His church. He's describing the legal basis for the New Covenant that God has been promising to Israel through the prophets. It is the reality of this New Covenant, the binding contract that God made with mankind through the blood of Jesus, which constitutes what is *bound in Heaven*. Think of how a binding contract or covenant works. If someone breaches that contract, what are the consequences, and how are those consequences enforced? What sorts of people get involved in that enforcement process? How important is it for those people to know the details of that contract?

4. There is much understanding to be gained by comparing the function of a government or legal system in a nation with your role as a key-keeper in the government of God. But the final aspect of binding and loosing that you need to see today is their dependence on the power of your *declarations*. Your speech enforces the covenant you have with God.

   A. Look at **Psalm 107:20** and **Luke 4:35,39**. How would you describe the role of the spoken word of God in these verses? Why is it important that Jesus verbally rebuked the demons or sickness?

   B. Now look at **John 14:10**. Do you see the connection that Jesus makes between speaking under God's authority and God Himself *doing* the works?

JOURNAL/MEDITATION

*Some kinds of safety deposit boxes require two keys
to turn simultaneously in order to open them. This is a
picture of binding and loosing. God has already put His
keys in all the doors of heaven, so to speak, and opened
some and shut others. As you learn of these doors through
revelation, you have been given keys—declarations—with
which to agree with what you see in heaven. When you
say what the Father is saying and do what He is doing, as
Jesus did, you open the doors of heavenly reality into earth.*

*So the question is, what is God saying today? If He
gives you or has already given you a promise or a word
for any particular situation you are facing, turn that into
a declaration. Speak it out loud! Declare those things that
stand against the Word of the Lord to be **bound by the
blood of Jesus**, and declare the reality of the Word to be
loosed from Heaven into your present circumstances.*

*And, just for fun, try making a list of how many things
we're called to do as Christians that involve our voices.
Here's a start: Prayer, Praise, Confession....*

Revelation: We Perish Without It

WHERE THERE IS NO VISION, THE PEOPLE PERISH... (Proverbs 29:18, KJV)

Revelation...opens up new realms of living, of possibility, of faith. It is absolutely impossible to live the normal Christian life without receiving regular revelation from God. The Bible says... *"My people are destroyed for lack of knowledge"* (Hos. 4:6). Proverbs 29:18 says similarly, *"Where there is no revelation, the people cast off restraint."* A more correct and complete translation is: "Without prophetic revelation, the people go unrestrained, walking in circles, having no certain destiny."

The biblical word *vision* doesn't mean "goals." Goals are fine, but this *vision* is referring to the spirit of revelation coming upon you, giving you a vision of things that are unseen.... Without unfolding prophetic revelation that expands your capacity to see life from God's perspective, you will perish. Without seeing your present circumstances through God's eyes, you will spiritually die.

(Quote from *The Supernatural Power of a Transformed Mind: Access to a Life of Miracles*, Pages 66-67.)

QUESTIONS

1. As today's verse says, your ability to walk through life with a "certain destiny" is only possible through prophetic revelation. This is significant, because there are a lot of people in the world who think they can find their destiny apart from prophetic revelation from God. But even the Son of God found His destiny through prophetic revelation. When Mary was told that her Son would be the Savior of God's people Israel, the implication was that Jesus' life would fulfill the pages of prophecies already given concerning the Messiah. That's a lot of destiny! One particular Messianic prophecy might provide some keys to today's subject. Read **Psalm 40:6-8**. Given that Jesus took on the limitations of man when He came to earth, it is likely that, beyond the prophetic word given to Mary and those surrounding His birth, He also discovered His identity as He studied the Scriptures while growing up. Therefore Christ fulfilled this prophecy in part by realizing that "in the scroll of the book it [was] written of" Him. Is it possible that God intends for you to discover your destiny in the Scriptures as well?

2. Look at what David discovered about his destiny in **Psalm 139:13-16**. What do you suppose is the "book" David refers to here? Considering that the Book of Moses was the only Scripture he knew, it wasn't necessarily the Bible. Isn't it intriguing that God would leave clues like this in the Bible about His *other* book, the book that contains the record of the lives of His saints in eternity? Is it possible that God could reveal His divine record of your life in eternity so you could live today in light of who you're meant to become?

3. It seems that the apostle Paul lived by pulling on the revelation of his destiny. Look at these familiar verses: **Philippians 3:12, 14**. Verse 14 in the New King James Version says, *"I press toward the goal."* How is this different from the fact that the vision you need isn't merely "goals"? How is *the* goal different from many goals?

4. The vision that you need is "prophetic revelation that expands your ability to see life from God's perspective." So "the goal" that you are to press on to really has to do with having your *worldview* shaped by a growing understanding of your identity and purpose in God as human beings on the planet. Eugene Peterson's *The Message* renders Proverbs 29:18 thus: *"If people can't see what God is doing, they stumble all over themselves, but when they attend to what He reveals, they are most blessed."* The vision you need is to see what God is doing: in the immediate present, in the contexts of history, and His revealed plan for mankind in Scripture.

JOURNAL / MEDITATION

The apostle Paul lived with one "goal": the "upward call of God in Christ Jesus." Because his life was only about one thing, he was able to tap into incredible power and revelation and did what no believer in the previous generation had accomplished: He spread the Gospel throughout a huge part of the known world. You may not feel like we are "perishing" without his level of focus, but the truth is, if you can't articulate our "one goal" and point to where each aspect of your life is intentionally "pressing on" to fulfill it, then you are likely to end up "walking in circles, having no certain destiny."

Today, ask the Holy Spirit to remind you of the vision that He has put in your heart. Then ask Him to shine His light on any area of your life where you are not pressing forward in that goal. If He shows you anything, don't panic or start striving. Simply ask Him for a plan to change what you're doing so you're moving in the right direction. He will show you!

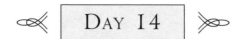

The Spirit of Revelation

B UT GOD HAS REVEALED THEM TO US THROUGH HIS SPIRIT. FOR THE SPIRIT SEARCHES ALL THINGS, YES, THE DEEP THINGS OF GOD. (1 Corinthians 2:10)

The Bible says the natural man does not *receive* the things of the Spirit of God.... The key is to be spiritually discerning—to open our spirit man to direct revelation from God.

The Holy Spirit searches for things that have never been heard by human ears or seen by human eyes. He is the greatest search engine in the whole universe. Talk about quick and accurate! He searches the greatest reservoir of information imaginable—the heart of the Father.... God has been around a long time, and He has had a long time to think about you.... For trillions of years, God has been thinking about you, and the Holy Spirit searches that whole archive and brings incredible treasures to you at precisely the right moment—if you're listening.

You'll know when He is speaking because it will have a freshness to it. It will always be better than anything you could have thought up yourself. And if He gives you new ideas, they will probably be impossible for you to accomplish in your own strength. His thoughts will so overwhelm you that you'll want to draw close to Him so they can be accomplished.

(Quote from *The Supernatural Power of a Transformed Mind:
Access to a Life of Miracles,* Pages 67-69.)

QUESTIONS

1. How often does it occur to you that God is always thinking about you? Do you ever feel like you have to get God's attention? Look at this promise in **Psalm 34:15, 17.** This is only one of many, many promises that the Lord gives: to be with you always. In fact, He sent His Spirit to live inside you! You can't get much closer than that.

2. So, if you feel unaware of His presence and voice, it is probably a matter of *listening.* And listening is, in the words of First Corinthians 2:14, *"spiritually discerning."* This is the job of your spirit man; so, in order to grow in listening, you must practice those activities which strengthen your spirit's ability to receive the things of the Spirit. Who better can show you how to do this than Jesus? Look at **Mark 1:35, Luke 5:16,** and **Luke 6:12.** What three places where Jesus prayed are mentioned in these verses? What do they have in common? Why is that environment conducive to listening? How often do you get away from everything to listen to God? Do you find it difficult? If so, why do you think that is?

3. Here are the keys to discerning the things that are from God and those that are from other voices. You know you're hearing God if what you're hearing is: (A) something you wouldn't have thought of on your own, and (B) something that is beyond your ability to accomplish. Can you remember something that you thought of or heard in your spirit that met these qualifications? How did you respond to it? Did you brush it off, thinking, "Dream on"? Did you recognize that "freshness" to the idea? Take a moment to remember it and ask the Holy Spirit if it was something He was giving to you.

4. The *natural* reaction to an impossibility is to feel overwhelmed and hopeless. But a person with renewed thinking has gained God's perspective on impossibilities: "His thoughts will so overwhelm you that you'll want to draw close to Him so they can be accomplished." Look again at the familiar passage in **Luke 1:26-38.** Did Mary "draw close" to the Lord to see His amazing words accomplished? If God can conceive His Son in the life of a teenage girl without any effort from her except her simple faith in His word, how will He not fail to conform you to the image of His Son as you also simply receive His words about you?

JOURNAL/MEDITATION

*Take some time to **listen** to God today. Ask the
Holy Spirit to renew in your mind and heart the
whispers of ideas and dreams that you have brushed
off as impossibilities. Ask Him to tell you some of God's
thoughts toward you, and be sure to write them down!
If He speaks a word of promise or destiny, draw near
to Him and ask Him, "How will this be?" As with Mary,
this isn't always a skeptical question, but can be one
of divine curiosity. If you have accepted Jesus, and the
Holy Spirit lives in you, the hunger to know Him
and His ways is at the truest, deepest part of you.*

Attracting Revelation

THROUGH WISDOM A HOUSE IS BUILT, AND
BY UNDERSTANDING IT IS ESTABLISHED; BY
KNOWLEDGE THE ROOMS ARE FILLED WITH ALL
PRECIOUS AND PLEASANT RICHES.

(Proverbs 24:3-4)

There are pillar truths in the gospel that form the most basic foundation of the structure. Once you have these in place, God delightfully adds to them, as a decorator decorates a house after the foundation and walls are secure. A man of understanding accepts God's additions and doesn't question them. He is not double-minded about them. That's how a person of understanding attracts greater understanding. You treasure something that God says, and that builds a foundation for greater revelation.

Another way to attract revelation is to obey what we know.... Obedience is a signal to God that says, "God, I want to go the next step." That tender heart draws the spirit of revelation to a person and/or body of people; they begin seeing and hearing things they never heard or saw before. The Bible even says, "*He will seal up that instruction in our heart in the night while we sleep*" (Job 33:15-16).

(Quote from *The Supernatural Power of a Transformed Mind: Access to a Life of Miracles*, Pages 69-70.)

QUESTIONS

1. Pillar truths are also called "core values," the foundational *statements of faith* that uphold the structure of a perspective or worldview. When you first embark on your journey as a disciple of Christ, you are intent on learning these foundational truths about God's nature and your identity and purpose in Him. If your enemy can't keep you from learning these truths, he works to make you believe that knowing *about* them is the goal of discipleship, not living them out from a deepening relationship with God Himself. If you value your connection with the Spirit of God more than anything, then growing in revelation will be more about getting to know the most amazing Friend and Father you've ever met than trying to measure up to some spiritual standard. Revelation comes through relationship. How is your value for your connection with the Holy Spirit expressed in your lifestyle? Do you feel you are growing in the revelation of who God is in your relationship with Him?

2. Jesus had some particular things to say about obedience, and most of them have to do with His conviction that obedience is first a matter of the heart. Read **John 14:21-26.**

   A. Do you think Jesus is setting up some kind of condition for loving Him, or is He merely describing how someone who loves Him will be identified? Would it be fair to say that He is describing obedience to His commands as the overflow of a heart that truly loves Him?

   B. Can you see how the obedience of a heart that loves God draws the abiding presence of Jesus and the Father? Would you say that this is a picture of how to attract revelation through obedience?

3. You may have noticed this about Christ's commands, but none of them can be practically applied at face value. More revelation is required in order to know what obedience looks like in your personal life. In this same speech in the Book of John, Jesus tells His disciples, *"Love one another as I have loved you"* (John 15:12). Can you see how you could use some more details to put that into action? Why do you suppose Christ gives commands like this? Could it be that He desires those details to be discovered through your relationship with Him? Is this perhaps why He promises the Holy Spirit's help in the same sentence about keeping His commands? How is this picture of obedience through relationship different from religious observance?

4. Now, as you walk out your relationship with God, He will ask you to do things that you don't understand fully. He's not asking you to prove yourself; He's asking you to trust Him! The man of understanding is a man of trust. This is why he can accept God's specific requests of him without questions. Have you stepped out in trust when you didn't understand God's reasons? What was the result?

JOURNAL/MEDITATION

Probing your heart to see if you love God enough is always a dead end. The point is that God is able to lead you into His heart of love and obedience, if you will trust Him. Pray David's prayer today: **"Search me, O God, and know my heart; try me, and know my anxieties; and see if there is any wicked way in me, and lead me in the way everlasting"** *(Ps. 139:23-24). Ask the Lord to deepen your ability to treasure what you have heard Him say to you, and ask how you can take the next step to bring your life into obedience with that.*

Broadening the
Playing Field of Faith

JESUS ANSWERED AND SAID TO THEM,
"ASSUREDLY, I SAY TO YOU, IF YOU HAVE FAITH
AND DO NOT DOUBT, YOU WILL NOT ONLY DO
WHAT WAS DONE TO THE FIG TREE, BUT ALSO IF
YOU SAY TO THIS MOUNTAIN, 'BE REMOVED AND
CAST INTO THE SEA,' IT WILL BE DONE."

(Matthew 21:21)

Revelation is for every single believer, not just for some "gifted" folks. The greater revelation that a person carries, the greater faith he or she is able to exercise. If I believe it's not God's desire to heal everybody then my revelation limits me every time a person comes to me who is sick. I have to settle it in my heart—is it really God's will to heal people? As long as I shun the revelation that God wants everybody to be healed and whole, I have cut myself off from releasing faith in that area. Revelation enlarges the arena that our faith can function in. Deception shrinks our area of faith.

...What if you realized that the lifestyle Jesus lived and taught is meant to be *your* lifestyle? Revelation would broaden the boundaries for your faith to operate in.

(Quote from *The Supernatural Power of a Transformed Mind: Access to a Life of Miracles*, Page 70.)

QUESTIONS

1. Do you find it easy to look at someone who is operating in greater faith, revelation, and power than you are and have your first response be something like, "Well, they must be special and I'm not" or "I could never do that"? If so, you'll notice that both of those responses are based on your self-perception. And because you are made in the image of God, your self-perception is directly related to your perception of who God is. This is why, when God came to men and women of Scripture and called them to do great exploits, He always revealed who *He was*, and said, "I will be with you." Look at two famous examples. Read **Exodus 3:1-14** and **Joshua 1:1-5**. What did God promise to Moses and Joshua? Why was that enough? How did this revelation of God enable these men to operate in a larger "playing field of faith"?

2. As a believer in Christ, you have God's promise not only that He will always be *with* you, but that He lives inside you by the Holy Spirit. This is why you have an entirely new identity. Read **Romans 8:14-21,29**. There is plenty to unpack from this passage, but what particular phrases does Paul use to describe your identity, now that you have received the Spirit? How does he indicate in verses 17 and 29 that from God's standpoint, His adopted children are considered just as legitimate as His only begotten Son, Jesus? What two things are going to be revealed in verses 18 and 19?

3. You are indeed called to live the lifestyle that Jesus taught and demonstrated, because you are co-heirs with Him and have been called to deliver creation from bondage! You know this because you have the same Holy Spirit in you that He had during His life on earth. But as you saw in the previous verses, that Holy Spirit gives you a particular cry to God. What is it? If the Holy Spirit moves you to address God so personally, what nature of relationship must you be invited to have with God? Remember, revelation comes through relationship. Can you see that as you grow in the personal knowledge of God through encountering Him, your faith grows?

JOURNAL/MEDITATION

Something that will keep you from expanding the playing field of your faith is failing to recognize that when God brings you into a new revelation or experience of His nature, He is not just giving you a taste of it, but He is inviting you to a deeper level of relationship where that aspect of His nature is expressed. For example, if He gives you a financial miracle, He is inviting you to know Him as your provider for every need you will possibly have in your life. If He lets you taste His incredible joy—which is your strength!—He is inviting you to a deeper relationship with Him where your life never lacks joy in any situation.

What has He done in your life recently? Respond to His invitation to know Him more deeply. Let the revelation of His goodness in a single situation enlarge your faith so you can partner with Him to release that part of His nature in your life and to those around you.

Living With Mystery

IT IS THE GLORY OF GOD TO CONCEAL A MATTER, BUT THE GLORY OF KINGS IS TO SEARCH OUT A MATTER. (Proverbs 25:2)

❧ TODAY'S DEVOTION ❧

Revelation is locked up in the realm called mystery. A mystery cannot be hunted down and trapped like an animal. It can't be discovered by persistent searching. It must be revealed. We don't unlock mysteries; they are unlocked for us. And they are only unlocked and revealed to those who hunger for them.

...Mystery should be a continual part of your life. You should always have more questions than answers. If your encounters with God don't leave you with more questions than when you started, then you have had an inferior encounter. A relationship with God that does not stir up that realm of mystery and wonder is an inferior relationship.

...We cannot afford to live only in what we understand because then we don't grow or progress anymore; we just travel the same familiar roads we have traveled all of our Christian life. It is important that we expose ourselves to impossibilities that force us to have questions that we cannot answer. It is a part of the Christian life, which is why the Christian life is called "the faith."

...This realm of mystery and revelation goes far beyond what we normally think of as "ministry." There are vast resources of revelation in heaven for the areas of education and business, the arts and music, and these resources have yet to be tapped anywhere near to their fullness.... Our job is to tap the revelation of the Lord in our area of talent or gifting so that we can accurately and powerfully reflect the King and His Kingdom.

(Quote from *The Supernatural Power of a Transformed Mind: Access to a Life of Miracles*, Pages 71-72, 75.)

QUESTIONS

1. If you like to read mystery stories, you know what it feels like to be drawn into the search for clues and the puzzle of reading the evidence. If you think about it, a mystery consists of something you do know (that a crime was committed, for example), and something you don't know (who committed the crime and how they did it). What you do know creates a powerful desire to discover what you don't know. That is the nature of mystery. Why do you think Scripture says the drive to know and understand hidden matters is *glorious*? What particular qualities does it bring out in a person? Do you think the desire to learn more about the world, ourselves, and God is innate in human beings? If so, how is that aspect of our nature part of the image of God, in which we were made?

2. Does the idea of living in mystery—that is, living in the tension of what you do know and what you don't know—make you uncomfortable? Is it common for people to be afraid of the unknown? History tells us that when people made new discoveries that challenged the worldview of their generation they were often doubted and even persecuted. Humans don't like to find out that they have believed something false for centuries. Disillusionment often leads people to embrace skepticism and cynicism in order to protect themselves from being hoodwinked. But fear of deception is a deception in itself, because fear of anything but God is based on lies. Fear absolutely prevents us from being able to learn something new and "grow and progress." Look at **Matthew 13:11**. What do you suppose it means to "know the mysteries" of the Kingdom? Look at the phrase: "It has been given to you to know the mysteries." In other words, it is saying, "You get to know the mysteries." This is a promise of privilege, of access. Do you think that God gives you access to mysteries as an invitation to pursue them? If so, does embracing mystery as a essential element of your experience with God help you position yourself to stay aware of what you *don't know* as much as what you do know?

3. Read **Matthew 18:2-4**. According to verse 4, what particular quality that children possess does Jesus say you need to have? There is something about the humility of children that reveals what it means to live with mystery. Consider these aspects of the humility of children:
   A. Think about how children relate to the "mysterious," to what they don't know. Children ask lots of questions; they wonder about everything. That quality of wonder—or you could say "awe"—is the foundation of humility because it comes from a healthy understanding that you are small in a big world and you don't know everything! At the same time, there are so many wonderful things to discover!
   B. Children also have an amazing ability to trust and take risks to discover the world around them. If Daddy tells you to jump off the jungle gym into his

arms, you'll do it! This trust is what you need in order to jump into the unknown and let God lead you down new roads.

C.   Children are also very creative! They love making mud pies, fingerpainting, and playing games. This inventive, playful quality is part of their process of discovering the world. The mystery realm is a storehouse of creative revelations. Recovering a childlike humility to try things in the creative process builds a template for those revelations to show up on.

D.   Children also live with a sense of timelessness about life. They aren't at the mercy of the clock; they are fully present with whatever is going on. Failing to be present is often what costs you your ability to see into the mystery realm—to notice things you never see when you're rushing around.

JOURNAL/MEDITATION

Children know how to live in mystery. Their encounters with the world always leave them with more questions than answers. Ask the Lord today to give you insight into how you can recover that mind-set of wonder, trust, creativity, and timelessness. Ask Him to teach you how to be fully present to what He is saying and doing, and to pick up the language of the Spirit speaking in unexpected ways. It's the glory of God to conceal a matter, because it provides the opportunity for you, whom He has called as a "king and priest," to seek them out. When you declare that He alone has the answers you seek, He is glorified, and so are you. He wants to teach you things you've never known.

Revelation Comes to the Desperate

LET US KNOW, LET US PURSUE THE KNOWL-EDGE OF THE LORD. (Hosea 6:3)

Picture a person desperate enough to open his or her heart fully and issue a deep cry from the spirit. That deep part of man calls to the deep part of God. That opening of the heart determines the level of revelation we receive. Few people I know receive substantial revelations or visitations of God without reckless pursuit.

…The spirit of revelation opens up our knowledge of who God is, and from that comes the release of power from heaven. That power gives us access to all things pertaining to life and godliness. That encounter with God will not only shape the world around you, it will shape the world *through* you.

…The cry of Hosea was, "Let's press on—no, let's hunt down and chase the encounter with God that changes our understanding of reality." That is the kind of relentless pursuit every believer should have about the things of God.

(Quote from *The Supernatural Power of a Transformed Mind: Access to a Life of Miracles,* Pages 72-74.)

QUESTIONS

1. What causes you to recklessly pursue God? Read **Matthew 5:3,6**. These are probably familiar verses, but that doesn't mean they're easy to understand. What does it mean to be poor in spirit?

    A. Take a look at some of the uses of "poor" in Strong's Concordance: "begging; destitute of wealth, influence, position, or honor; lowly; afflicted; destitute of the Christian virtues and eternal riches; powerless to accomplish an end."

    B. Interestingly, the root word for "hunger" in verse 6 also means "poor," and "thirst" means to "painfully feel the want of" something. So would it be fair to say that being "poor in spirit" and "hungering and thirsting for righteousness" are describing someone who is keenly aware of their desperate need for God? Does this describe you?

2. Have you noticed that when you are hungry it is very difficult to focus on anything besides food? There is something about desperate need that eliminates distractions. David was a man who was keenly aware of his need for God. Many times he tells the Lord in the Psalms, "I am poor and needy" (Ps. 40:17; 70:5; 86:1; 109:22). David had everything in terms of wealth, and he walked in a relationship and revelation of God that far surpassed any other in the Old Testament. But his desperation for God produced the "deep cries" that touched the heart of God and gave him the key to enter into that revelation. Read **Psalm 27:4**. Do you have "one thing" that you desire of the Lord, and "one thing" you are seeking? Is that one thing producing a cry of desperation in you? If you don't feel like you have that singular focus in your life, then honestly consider your awareness of your need for God. Is your awareness great enough to be producing "deep cries" to Him from your heart? Is it moving you to take risks or do extreme things to get more of Him?

3. True hunger isn't something you can turn on and off. But there are things you can do to help strip away the distractions that keep you from that single vision and help you regain our awareness of our hunger and need for God. Read **Matthew 6:22**. Some translations say, "If your eye is single, your whole body will be full of light." When you focus your gaze solely on the Lord, your whole life is transformed by His light. Spiritual disciplines like fasting, solitude, silence, or retreats are tools for helping you develop that single focus. By eliminating distractions and focusing solely on God, you stir up and feed your connection with God. This is where you "behold the beauty of the Lord." Can you remember the last time you saw something so beautiful that it was awesome to behold? What did you feel? Do you recognize the things that move you in the deep places of your heart? Have you been moved like that in the presence of God?

4. "The knowledge of God" is not knowledge *about* Him. It is only knowledge that comes through encountering His presence. It is the knowledge of relationship. Because it is true that you become like that which you behold, it is the deep knowing in your relationship with God that produces increased access to the divine nature and power that changes you and the world around you. If you learn how to stay aware of your desperate need for God, which produces the deep cries in your heart that draw Him to you, that desperation eventually becomes a passionate longing and love for God. And love is the highest, purest motive you can live from. Do you recognize the difference between living from love and living from poverty of spirit?

JOURNAL/MEDITATION

Ask the Lord to speak to you today about having and living from the "one thing" that you desire and seek in your relationship with Him. Ask Him to show you the steps to take to eliminate any distractions that are dulling your passion for Him. Then ask Him to take you into a deeper revelation of His manifest presence, where you behold His beauty and where the things that move Him move you more deeply.

Revelation Is an Invitation to Experience

Y OU SEARCH THE SCRIPTURES, FOR IN THEM YOU THINK YOU HAVE ETERNAL LIFE; AND THESE ARE THEY WHICH TESTIFY OF ME. BUT YOU ARE NOT WILLING TO COME TO ME THAT YOU MAY HAVE LIFE. (John 5:39-40)

Y ou see, renewing the mind is not merely reading words on a page and having a moment of revelation about a particular verse. That passes for renewal of the mind in many churches, but at best that's only half the equation. Renewal comes as revelation leads you into a new experience with God.

...Jesus put it this way in John 5:39: "*You search the Scriptures, for in them you think you have eternal life; and these are they which testify of Me.*" This says clearly that revelation is meant to bring us to an encounter with God, and if it doesn't, it only makes us more religious.... To renew the mind we must not just *think* differently but *live* differently, in a new experience of the empowerment of the Holy Spirit.

...Revelation should change our hearts before we could ever explain what we learned. The Bible says we are, as a matter of fact, seated at the right hand of the Father in Christ Jesus in heavenly places. This was written for us to experience, not so we have good theology, not so that our doctrinal statements are accurate and concise. Statements like this are launching pads into encounters where we experience the very things that are on the page.

(Quote from *The Supernatural Power of a Transformed Mind: Access to a Life of Miracles*, Pages 80, 84.)

QUESTIONS

1. The story of Israel is a rich example of what happens when you choose religion—which is focused on knowing *about* God—over an experiential relationship with God. Read **Exodus 20:18-21**. How did Israel perceive God's motives toward them? How did Moses perceive God's motives? Why do you think the Israelites and Moses had differing perspectives?

2. God's original desire for the people of Israel was for them all to be His priests (see Exod. 19:6). But because Israel consistently chose to disobey God and depend on mediators like Moses and Joshua to speak to God for them, they never experienced what God intended for them. But God restored their opportunity for relationship with Him through the New Covenant in Jesus' blood. Read **Jeremiah 31:31-34**. The word in this passage for "know" in the Hebrew is *yada*, which means personal, experiential knowledge. In the New Covenant you have access to personal, intimate knowledge of God. You don't have to go through a mediator to find out what God is saying or wants because you have your heart and mind imprinted with who He is. Do you think that God's intention in making this covenant with you is to have only one initial encounter where you are forgiven and imprinted with His laws? If not, and if His intention was to have a lifelong, experiential relationship with every believer, do you think He would want you to expect daily interaction with Him? How is interaction different from religious observance—that is, what do prayer, worship, and devotions look like when they are part of a relationship, not duty?

3. You've already seen that people have a tendency to struggle when they see something in Scripture that they haven't yet experienced in their lives. Some disqualify themselves, thinking that they'll never measure up. Others make excuses for why that part of the Bible can't possibly apply to them. How do you shift your mind-set to see those places as invitations to grow to a new level of experience in your relationship with God? Take, for example, **First Thessalonians 5:16-18**. This passage is describing activities that are meant to be continuously present in your life, and verse 18 says they are what? Considering that the will of God is *"on earth as it is in heaven,"* could you say that these activities require heavenly reality and power to perform? Do you think you've experienced the fullness of this aspect of God's will in your life—that is, do you have continuous joy, communication with God, and thanksgiving occurring in your life? If not, could these verses be indicating that there is a greater measure of heaven that God has available for you to rise to that experience?

4. So how exactly do you step into experiencing the will of God in a greater measure? Remember that your mind is a gatekeeper that invites heavenly reality to be actualized in your experience. Agreement requires a particular faculty of your minds, which is your power to focus on something and meditate on it or *imagine* it. Your imagination helps you to *visualize* things, which is actually a kind of experience. Performing artists and athletes have found that rehearsing their music or game in their minds has almost the same benefit as if they had physically done it, because their imaginations allow them to have a certain level of experience. Take the passage from First Thessalonians again. How do you imagine your life would look if you were "rejoicing always"?

Write down your thoughts to the last question. Describe what your day would look like with continuous joy, prayer, and thanks in it. Describe what kind of prayers you would pray. Describe how it would affect your perspective on the issues facing you. Describe how it would affect your relationships with your family and your encounters with people in town or at work. As you visualize this, invite the Holy Spirit of revelation to open your eyes to the life that He has made available to you—proving the will of God in Christ Jesus for you.

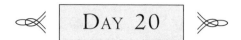
Falling Short of Experience

WHEN ANYONE HEARS THE WORD OF THE
KINGDOM, AND DOES NOT UNDERSTAND
IT, THEN THE WICKED ONE COMES AND
SNATCHES AWAY WHAT WAS SOWN IN HIS HEART.

(Matthew 13:19)

The revelation of the Kingdom is often spoken of as a living seed of another world that carries with it new possibilities. But when a person hears the word but doesn't understand it, the enemy has open access to that seed and can snatch it away. In our culture, we define understanding as nothing more than cognitive reasoning, coming to conclusions, fully comprehending. But in Eastern culture, which is the culture of Scripture, understanding is an *experience*. It means engaging in activities that involve our five senses. In fact, the Greek word for *understanding* in this verse means "learning which takes place through the five senses." It means *doing*, as in *practical human experience*. The biblical view of understanding means far more than to give mental assent; it means to practice in real life what one has come to know by revelation.

...Revelation takes us only halfway there; experience leads us all the way. The great tragedy is that if you don't move into experience, that revelation remains locked in your mind so you think it's active in your life. ...Hearing without doing has locked you into a form without power.

(Quote from *The Supernatural Power of a Transformed Mind: Access to a Life of Miracles*, Pages 82-83.)

QUESTIONS

1. If you went to a doctor who told you he had read all the books on a particular surgery but had never actually performed one, would you want him to work on you? Would you take your car to a mechanic who had studied every car design in existence but had never worked on an actual car? This is the kind of "experience" that you need in your relationship with God—the only thing that will produce real "fruit" in your life, according to the parable in Matthew 13. Read **Matthew 13:18-23**. What is the "fruit" that Jesus is talking about? How is a tangible, measurable result of the Word of the Kingdom in your life different from hearing the Word and receiving it? What do the different types of "ground" symbolize?

2. Every experience you have with God will be an experience with His *grace*. Grace is God's unmerited favor, but it also refers to His power. As you've seen, without power, the gospel is not good news. You need God's power not only to perform miracles, but to *know Him*. Read **Ephesians 3:14-19**. Paul prays for God to grant that you be strengthened by the Holy Spirit in your inner man for three main purposes. Why do you need power for Christ to dwell in your heart through faith? Why do you need power to comprehend the love of God that surpasses knowledge, and how can you know something beyond knowledge? Why do you need power to be filled with the fullness of God?

3. You also can't be called a "witness" of God without personal experience. Read **Acts 1:8**. Notice the order of events. What had to happen before the disciples would be witnesses? Earlier in the Gospels, Jesus had commissioned His disciples to minister in power, and they witnessed great things. Why did they have to have this new experience at Pentecost in order to be witnesses?

4. You also can't have fellowship with the saints without experience! Read **First John 1:1-3**. Notice how many times John refers to the personal, sensory interaction with Jesus. He—and those he is writing for—has seen Jesus, heard Jesus, and touched Jesus. In verse 3, he gives the reason for declaring his testimony of personal experience. What is it? Why is so important to realize that what you truly have in common with other believers is personal experience with Christ, more than agreement over the same issues? Is that the focus in your fellowship with other believers?

JOURNAL / MEDITATION

*Falling short of experiencing what is revealed to you means falling short of everything you need to truly live the Christian life. It is your personal encounters with God that impart to you the divine grace you need to know His love, be His witness, and share in the community of the saints. As some might say of a particular skill, the grace of God is **caught** as much as it is taught. And you only catch it when you hang around in His presence, hearing His voice, seeing Him move, feeling His touch. God never expects you to have a relationship with Him where you don't have regular hands-on experience with His presence and love, just as you would never marry someone you would never see or live with. Invite His Holy Spirit to highlight one area today in your relationship with Him where He wants to let you experience His love that surpasses knowledge.*

The Process of Understanding

B Y FAITH WE UNDERSTAND…

(Hebrews 11:3)

TODAY'S DEVOTION

To understand also means yielding to something before you can explain, define, or describe it. Biblical understanding far surpasses the intellect. Hebrews 11:3 says, *"By faith we understand that the worlds were framed by the word of God, so that the things which are seen were not made of things which are visible."* We don't have faith because we understand, but we understand because we have faith.... Biblical learning takes place in the spirit first, and as we obey the Spirit of God, our spirit communicates it to our minds so we intellectually understand. But understanding is not required for obedience. A normal Christian is one who *obeys the revelations and promptings of the Holy Spirit without understanding.* Understanding usually unfolds in the experience.

(Quote from *The Supernatural Power of a Transformed Mind: Access to a Life of Miracles,* Pages 82-83.)

QUESTIONS

1. Jesus clearly linked faith with understanding as He taught His disciples. Read **Matthew 16:5-11**. There are three main questions that Jesus asks here, and He asks them inductively. Look at them in a backward order:

   A. *"How is it that you do not understand that I did not speak to you concerning bread?"* The immediate context is that Jesus' disciples have just completely misunderstood His warning about the leaven of the Pharisees and Sadducees.

   B. *"Do you not yet understand, or remember the five loaves of the five thousand and how many loaves you took up? Nor the seven loaves of the four thousand and how many large baskets you took up?"* Jesus' implication here is that if they had *understood* what happened in these miracles, the issue of them not bringing bread would never have occurred as a possible response to His warning.

   C. *"O you of little faith, why do you reason among yourselves because you have brought no bread?"* Jesus goes right to the root of the issue first—the disciples lacked faith, which prevented them from understanding the miracle and therefore from understanding His warning. How does Jesus' perspective resonate with today's verse in Hebrews?

2. Without faith, the disciples' reasoning led them to ask the wrong questions and come to wrong conclusions. The same principle is true for you. The study of logic shows that every line of reasoning begins with an assumption—a statement of faith. If your assumption is wrong, your whole logic will be on a faulty foundation. So how do you make sure your assumptions are based on God's perspective? Look again at **Hebrews 11:1**. What two categories of "things" does faith relate to? Did you know that these are two different words in Greek?

   A. *"Faith is the substance of things hoped for."* Hope is not wishing; it is literally the "joyful expectation of good." So the "things hoped for" are all "goods" that you expect when you have faith. Do you wake up every morning with the confident expectation of good things? What are they?

   B. *"Faith is the...evidence of things not seen."* The "things not seen" are all "acts" or "deeds"—the activities of the unseen realm. So faith is the "evidence"— the "conviction" or "proof"—of what's going on in the unseen realm. As God works in the unseen on your behalf, your faith, which is your confidence and trust in Him, should continue to grow. Can you see how a carnal mind-set, focused on the natural world and its limitations, would hinder the growth of faith, since your faith depends on perceiving the unseen?

C. Check out how *The Message* puts Hebrews 11:1: *"The fundamental fact of existence is that this trust in God, this faith, is the firm foundation under everything that makes life worth living. It's our handle on what we can't see."*

3. If you don't have a faith that is built on the expectation of good and the perception of the unseen, then you won't be able to truly understand what God is doing in the world around you and what your purpose is. But the more you exercise your trust in God through obedience, the more that expectation and perception will grow, as will *your understanding*. Read **Isaiah 11:2**. How is "understanding" related to the Holy Spirit? Could it be that your understanding grows as you obey because the Holy Spirit increases in you as you obey?

4. Read **First Corinthians 1:26**. Why do you suppose this is true?

JOURNAL/MEDITATION

*Most believers came to Christ with little more
understanding of the truth than the simple truth that
they were sinners in need of God's forgiveness, which Christ
had paid for on the Cross. Virtually all of your understanding
of what you had really done in confessing your sin and
inviting Christ to come into your heart lay on the other side
of those acts of faith. But have you noticed that those who
come to Christ for forgiveness but are not willing to embark
on the journey of obedience to Christ do not come into
fuller understanding of salvation and most often fall away?*

*If you have pursued a life of obedience, you have probably
attained enough understanding of salvation and who
God is that the thought of turning from Him seems absurd.
But you only gained that understanding by taking
those consistent steps to trust Him. Ask the Lord
where you can trust Him more today.*

DAY 22

Establishing Revelation

NOW TO HIM WHO IS ABLE TO ESTABLISH YOU... ACCORDING TO THE REVELATION OF THE MYSTERY KEPT SECRET SINCE THE WORLD BEGAN....   (Romans 16:25)

When revelation is put into practice by one person, or one church, or the entire Body of Christ, it becomes more powerful than anything on earth. Take the concept of salvation by faith. For hundreds of years, beginning during the days of the Roman Empire, the Church did not understand or have assurance of salvation. This revelation was lost. But a few hundred years ago, the Church began to have a revelation of salvation by faith, even though it still was not easy for people to get saved. Many sincere people would seek God, pray, and search the Scriptures sometimes for weeks or even months before feeling some assurance that they had been saved. But because the Church embraced the revelation of salvation wholeheartedly, teaching it, practicing it, building up people's faith in it, today we consider it the simplest thing in the world.... Today we are riding on a wave of a heritage of faith that has increased for many generations.

A similar thing has happened with worship. ...Our understanding of this revelation has come through experience and practice, and the church's mind has been renewed.

The revelation of healing is on a similar trajectory....

(Quote from *The Supernatural Power of a Transformed Mind:*
Access to a Life of Miracles, Pages 85-86.)

QUESTIONS

1. Take a look at part of Jesus' strategy for establishing His revelation in the earth. Read **Matthew 28:18-20**. What two activities does He specify for His disciples to do in "making disciples"? What are you to teach disciples? How is teaching them to observe Christ's commands different from simply teaching them the commands?

   A. "Observing" Christ's commands has three dimensions to it.
      (1) It means to "see, or behold" them;
      (2) to "guard, or protect" them;
      (3) and to "practice" them.
   B. What has to happen for you to "see, or behold" Christ's commands? What has to happen for you to teach disciples how to do the same? What must you do to "guard or protect" Christ's commands? How do you teach disciples to do the same? What must you do to "practice" Christ's commands? How do you teach disciples to do the same?

2. Christ's commission requires each believer to consistently do what He commanded, to study, memorize, teach, and preach it, and to *show*—not just tell—new disciples how to do those, as well as how to teach others themselves. The apostles of the early Church held the task of teaching disciples *how to teach* as a priority. Read **Second Timothy 2:2**.

   A. Have you ever heard that teaching something forces you to learn it more deeply? Why do you suppose that is?

   B. Do you trust teachers who don't practice what they preach? Why is modeling an essential element to teaching?

   C. How often are you aware that your words and behavior are setting an example for those around you? When you are aware of that, how does it affect you? When you came to Christ, were those who taught you and modeled Christian behavior for you aware of their responsibility to train you to not only imitate them, but to teach others to imitate you?

3. All of Christ's commands to practice supernatural ministry remained in Scripture, but the practice and modeling of it ceased in much of the Church. Perhaps the reason for this has to do with a breakdown in the other aspect of "observing" Christ's commands—the "guarding" and "protecting" aspect. Something is usually protected when it has value and when it is threatened. Failure to appreciate the value of what Christ taught and failure to understand the schemes of the enemy will always lead to a failure to observe it and teach others to observe it. The Book of Galatians is one of the many warnings in the Epistles against false

teachers who would try to create a breach in observing Christ's commands. Read **Galatians 1:6-9.**

A.   Now, "gospel" means "good news," so the false teachers who were coming to the Galatians were not leading the believers astray with blatant evil. They were trying to convince them that in order to please God they still had to keep certain laws. Have you noticed that the enemy usually tries to lure you away from the truth with the promise of "good"? Do you find it easy to slip into "religious mode" from a desire to please God and do the right things?

B.   Paul exposes the true motives of the false teachers in Galatians 6:12: They only wanted to avoid being persecuted for the cross of Christ. Do you think that the fear of offense and persecution has been at work where there has been a decline in the practice and teaching of the supernatural ministry of Christ?

JOURNAL/MEDITATION

*As we read in our verse for today, God is able to establish
you according to the revelation of the mystery of Christ.
God is able to heal His Church from the centuries-long
breach in observing Christ's commands and restore the
revelation and practice of the "everything" Christ
commissioned you to do and teach. Remember, all
of God's commands can only truly be kept in a daily
relationship with Him where you see what He is doing and
hear what He is saying. Invite the Spirit of revelation to come
and establish your understanding of Christ's revelation both
in your reading and daily practice as you walk with Him.*

DAY 23

The Fear of Excess

WHEN THE SON OF MAN COMES, WILL HE
REALLY FIND FAITH ON THE EARTH?

(Luke 18:8b)

Part of what holds us back is our concern with being excessive. We don't want people to think we're religious nuts; we fear excess much more than we fear lack. So many Christians avoid the subject of healing. You've probably heard a brother or sister in the Lord say, "You should read this book. It's really good, but be careful because the guy has a strange doctrine on such-and-such a point." People love to add warnings. But has anyone ever given you a tape or book and said, "This guy's teaching is great, but be careful because he has never raised the dead. Cancer doesn't leave people's bodies when he prays"? No, because as a body we lack experiential understanding of the revelation of healing and the supernatural.

When you put a revelation into practice, you won't get it 100 percent right. You might not even get it 50 percent right. But you will learn, and you will grow into a level of maturity you wouldn't otherwise have. At our church, the only way we know to learn is to experiment.

...Jesus had one concern about His return and it wasn't that He would find people who were excessive. Rather, He said, "*I tell you that He will avenge them speedily. Nevertheless, when the Son of Man comes, will He really find faith on the earth?*" (Luke 18:8). When you put your revelation into practice, what used to be impossible will look logical.

(Quote from *The Supernatural Power of a Transformed Mind: Access to a Life of Miracles*, Pages 87-89.)

QUESTIONS

1. There are several reasons why people are afraid of being excessive, and one has to do with fear of man and man-pleasing.

   A. Underlying the fear of man is usually the fear of punishment or persecution. This same fear was what influenced the Judaizers to attempt to coerce the Galatians into law-keeping. Look at Paul's response to them in **Galatians 6:14**. What does it mean to be crucified to the world? What does it mean that the world is crucified to you? How does having your identity totally wrapped up in the Cross and your focus completely focused on pleasing God affect your attitude toward persecution or the opinions of others?

   B. In Acts 4, the apostles experience persecution from the religious leaders for healing the man at the Beautiful Gate. Read their response to the threats in **Acts 4:18-20**. Would you say that if you have a real encounter with the power of God and/or minister in the power of God, there's a chance you'll be perceived as excessive? How does having a true testimony of experiencing God change your perspective so that you *cannot help* but share what God has done and invite others to experience Him too? Do you feel like you listen to God more than other voices?

   C. Man-pleasing can also manifest as a false compassion. When you walk in the Spirit, often He does a good job at what Jesus sent Him to do—to convict the world of sin, righteousness, and judgment (see John 16:8)—and that can make people uncomfortable. The challenge is to learn how to show kindness without minimizing what God is doing in order to ease someone's discomfort. In fact, the other part of the Spirit's job description is that *He* is the Comforter—and He does the best job at it. Look at Simon Peter's convicting experience in **Luke 5:4-11**. Why did Peter respond to Jesus the way he did? Why is it convicting to experience God's miraculous power and goodness? Look at Jesus' response: He simply pointed Peter to his true calling. How does this show true kindness and love rather than trying to make people feel better?

2. The fear of excess can rise up when you face the fact that God wants to bring you into greater encounters with Him than what you've experienced. Stepping out in faith can feel like "performing"—like you aren't being true to yourself. There is a righteous desire for truth and authenticity in the hearts of most believers, but what some have failed to do is define themselves in agreement with what God says about them more than anyone else.

   A. Look at a classic example of how God defines people according to His call, not their self-perceptions. Read **Judges 6:11-16**. What does the Lord call Gideon in verse 12? What does Gideon call himself in verse 15? Why are these two perspectives so different? Which one is truer? What two things does the Lord say to Gideon about what *He* has done and will do, in verses

14 and 16? Why are God's presence and God's "sending" in your life the main ingredients you need to fulfill your calling?

B. So how do you step into what God says about you, even if you don't get it 100 percent right at first? Let's look at Paul's instruction to the Corinthians in **First Corinthians 11:1**. Imitate means to "mimic." A lot of people feel uncomfortable mimicking others, whether it's playing a game of charades or trying anything new that someone is teaching you to do. But unless you step past your comfort zone, you never learn anything new! Does it make you uncomfortable to think about "imitating Christ," especially since He exhibited some pretty radical behavior? Does it feel like a stretch to believe that you could love people as well or as much as He did? What do you think Jesus expects of someone who truly wants to follow Him? Do you think He's pleased when we try to do what He asks, even if we only get it 50 percent right at first?

*In order to imitate someone, you have to pay close attention to them and not just **see**, but **study** the way they operate, and then **practice** doing what they do. At first it feels awkward and unnatural, but only with practice will it eventually become second nature to you. Paul tells us in Galatians that when you were baptized, you **"put on Christ"** (Gal. 3:27). You didn't just lose the filth of sin in the water; you were clothed with Him. The faith that Jesus is hoping to see when He returns is the faith of disciples who watch Him and practice being like Him because they believe they are already wearing Him—they just need to grow into Him! This is the mystery that Paul talks about in Second Corinthians 3:18; that you behold **"as in a mirror"** the glory of the Lord, and as you behold Him, you are being transformed **"into His likeness"** from glory to glory.*

Today, spend some time being still, and behold Jesus with your heart, mind, and body. Ask Him to speak to you and draw you into the revelation of what moved His heart and enabled Him to keep an undivided focus on His Father during His ministry. Then receive the grace He wants to give you to step out and do what He is doing today.

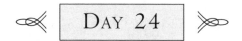

Learning From Supernatural Experiences

F OR THEY HAD NOT UNDERSTOOD ABOUT THE LOAVES, BECAUSE THEIR HEART WAS HARDENED. (Mark 6:52)

Miracles can be dazzling and dramatic, but they are not primarily designed to dazzle us. God gives us miracles to train us how to see differently.

...[The disciples] had obeyed perfectly when carrying out the miracle of the loaves and fishes, yet their hearts still remained hard. They hadn't seen through the miracle. It had not transformed them. You and I can obey God perfectly, and be the instrument that brings about the miracle and still have a hard heart through it and after it. It doesn't mean you're going to hell, but that you missed the lesson of the miracle.

What was the [disciple's] lesson? They should have seen their role in the miracle. Because they didn't see their role in the previous miracle, the next time they encountered a problem and Jesus wasn't in the boat, they had no solution.... They did not extract the nutrients from the last miracle. That hardness of heart prevented them from becoming deliverers, and so Jesus had to deliver them once again.

(Quote from *The Supernatural Power of a Transformed Mind:*
Access to a Life of Miracles, Pages 92-94.)

1. When you hear the phrase "hardness of heart" you may think of someone who is *heart-less*, rebellious, cold, and cynical. That is actually the extreme *result* of hardness of heart. More fundamentally, hardness of heart has to do with a *lack of ability to perceive and understand unseen reality from God's perspective.* Romans 1 provides a clear explanation of how we become hard-hearted. Read **Romans 1:18-25.**

    A. This is a passage packed with meaning, and it could be argued that this is the one of the clearest descriptions in Scripture of how and why you need your mind renewed. Look at these particular phrases:

        (1) *"His invisible attributes are clearly seen, being understood by the things that are made...."* The words "clearly seen" actually mean "seen from above." This phrase is saying that God's perspective on reality, His worldview, can be perceived in the total work of creation! There is a testimony in nature of who God is and what His purposes are. If you don't perceive this, the Bible says you have a hard heart. Do you perceive the beauty and purpose of God in creation? Do you perceive it in human beings?

        (2) *"... although they knew God, they did not glorify Him as God, nor were thankful...."* When you truly perceive God's invisible attributes and His perspective, there is only one way to respond: thanksgiving and worship. Do these two activities primarily characterize your response to God on a daily basis?

        (3) *"...became futile in their thoughts...."* "Futile" means "purposeless." Because your purpose as a human being can only be perceived within the structure of God's plan for creation, you lose purpose when you diverge from His perspective. "Thoughts" refers not just to individual thoughts, but to your way of thinking about yourself and reality—your mind-set or worldview. Do you feel like you understand your purpose within the big picture of God's design for creation and mankind?

        (4) *"... and their foolish hearts were darkened."* When your way of thinking is off, then your heart, which is the seat of your affections and desires, becomes dark—that is, you stop being drawn toward God and start being drawn away to lesser gods, whether it is yourself, another person, an object, or an activity. You can tell how much your mind is renewed by what your affections are drawn to, and *especially by what you turn to for comfort.* When you face difficult situations or even simple discomfort (e.g., when you're tired or stressed), what do you turn to? If it isn't the Holy Spirit, could you have another comforter that is sometimes more important than the Comforter?

    B. The more your mind is renewed, the more the "invisible attributes" of God and His divine purposes will become clear to you, particularly *His purpose to have a relationship with you.* This relationship is what will help you to not only obey God, but look for the revelation of His nature in your encounters with Him and expect them to prepare you for the next adventure with Him. This is what the disciples missed. Why do you think Jesus gave His disciples a role in the miracle of the loaves? Obviously He had more in mind for them to learn than mere obedience. What do you think they were meant to learn about their relationship with God from the miracle?

To put together a few truths that you've seen in the study so far, look at this progression: Revelation is intended as an invitation to encounter and experience. Understanding unfolds in the experience. But the lesson today adds that, without further revelation and the establishment of the pillars of God's perspective in your thinking, you can experience God and miss the fullness of understanding. So, in order to grow and mature in your relationship with God, there will need to be a continual dialogue, as it were, between revelation and experience.

God is calling you to maturity as His son or daughter. Good parents do not want their children to remain dependent on them for everything; rather, they want them to develop their own thinking and initiative in order to uphold their end of a reciprocal relationship. God wants nothing less from you. How is God calling you to make decisions from your heart? How is He giving you a role in the ministry He's called you to? Have you recognized that as an invitation to a deeper relationship with Him?

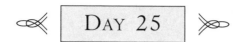
The Leaven of Herod and the Pharisees

THE JEWS REQUEST A SIGN AND THE GREEKS SEEK AFTER WISDOM; BUT WE PREACH CHRIST CRUCIFIED, TO THE JEWS A STUMBLING BLOCK AND TO THE GREEKS FOOLISHNESS.

(1 Corinthians 1:22–23)

Leaven is a picture of influence on our minds. Leaven in the natural realm causes dough to rise. My wife used to make bread, and if the bread wasn't rising, we would set it by the wood stove, and the heat would activate the leaven. The fire of difficulty similarly causes the leaven in your life to be exposed and brought to the surface.

...The leaven of Herod is an atheistic influence based on the strength of man and man-based systems, like politics, popular will, and persuasion. Herod's leaven excludes God entirely. Its statement of faith is a cynical, "God helps those who help themselves." ...Large numbers of Christians are practical atheists who disbelieve in an active God. They wouldn't say it that way; no church's written doctrine would declare there is no God. But believers face situations daily without bringing God into the picture.

...Pharisee leaven represents the religious system. It embraces God in theory but not in practice or experience.... Pharisees provide explanations, not solutions.

....Jesus exposes the core characteristic of the influences of Herod and the Pharisees: Both are based on the fear of man. Both are primarily motivated by what people think. But when we are influenced by Kingdom leaven, we don't fear what people think about us.

(Quote from *The Supernatural Power of a Transformed Mind: Access to a Life of Miracles*, Pages 95-97.)

QUESTIONS

1. Difficulty exposes that in which you actually *trust*, and what you trust is what we truly believe to be true and real. Look at what the "fire of difficulty" exposed in King Saul in **First Samuel 13:6-14**. In whom or what did Saul actually trust? Do you see the fear of man operating here? Which of the leavens is influencing Saul? What would have happened if he had trusted and obeyed God, according to Samuel? Have you ever been in a difficult situation and started scrambling to make something happen when it seemed God wasn't going to show up in time? What were the consequences?

2. God addresses what it looks like to embrace Him in theory but not practice (the leaven of the Pharisees) in **Isaiah 58**. Read the chapter and consider the following questions.

   A. How is telling God that you want Him and even doing something sacrificial, like fasting, different from the "practices" you should embrace if you are to truly embrace Him as our living, intervening God?

   B. Is God saying that you shouldn't practice spiritual disciplines like fasting and confession? Jesus practiced these things, so why was the fruit of Jesus' life different from the Pharisees'?

   C. How is caring for the poor and working to bring justice fasting? From what does it require you to abstain? How does this focus on bringing *solutions* to problems versus explanations?

   D. Why is doing spiritual things instead of the things God has asked you to do based on the fear of man? How does it betray a trust in man, especially man's reasoning, more than a real trust in and obedience to God?

3. Look at what Proverbs says about the fear of man in **Proverbs 29:25**. This verse may seem obvious, but it is powerful when you really believe it. The word "safe" literally means "to be set inaccessibly high." When you trust in and lean on God when difficulty comes, you will be above the reach of any scheme or lie of the enemy. Don't you want to be untouchable in difficulty? Are you currently facing any difficult circumstances? Do you recognize what exactly you are trusting in to help you? Is it your own or someone else's ability to make things happen? Is it in your ability to bring the correct spiritual diagnosis to the situation? Or is it in God's power and revelation to bring the solution or breakthrough you need?

Though Herod and the Pharisees aren't necessarily around today, their leavens most definitely are. Jesus has given you a powerful tool of discernment in defining the two primary anti-Kingdom ways of thinking that you face in the world. As you read the newspaper, watch TV, and talk with people about their perspectives, ask yourself which of these two leavens is at work behind the message.

In your experience, have you noticed that many Christians whom you know could be called "practical atheists" in terms of the degree to which they interact with God and are following Him through life? How have they fallen prey to the "trap" of the fear of man? Ask the Holy Spirit to show you how to pray for and speak to them and how to more fully follow Him yourself.

Where Does Your Thought Life Begin?

"**W**HY ARE YOU SO FEARFUL? HOW IS IT THAT YOU HAVE NO FAITH?" (Mark 4:40)

Today's Devotion

Jesus warned against Herod's and the Pharisees' leavens because they work against the renewal of our minds. In the immediate context when Jesus spoke these words, the great failure of the disciples was that they were afraid because they didn't pack a lunch, and Jesus had multiplied food for them twice. Their thought life began with what they lacked, and so they contradicted the revelation God had just given them about supernatural provision. They built their thought life on the improper foundation.

...I wish my first response to adversity was always to have faith. Sometimes it takes me a day or two, sometimes only a few minutes to get my heart and mind right. There are times when I get so troubled, so provoked and anxious, and I know biblically there is no reason for it. I always wonder, how can I be so worried and bogged down by pressures when He bought me with a price, gave me His Son, and will freely give me all things? Only because the leaven of Herod or the Pharisees has worked its way into my soul, and the pressure caused the leaven to rise.

Kingdom thinking knows that anything is possible at any time. It's activated when you and I with tender hearts surrender to the thought patterns of God, when we receive His imaginations and say "yes."

(Quote from *The Supernatural Power of a Transformed Mind: Access to a Life of Miracles*, Pages 98-100.)

1. The fear of lack is the foundation of a poverty mind-set, and like all fear, it is a deception that blinds you to what is true. The elder brother in Jesus' story about the prodigal son was under this mind-set. Read **Luke 15:25-32**.

   A. Does the elder brother see himself more as a servant or a son? Why does he think the younger brother is getting something that he doesn't get to have? What does the father say belongs to him?

   B. Do you think that if you fail to understand the relationship God has invited you into, you will fail to understand His provision? How does the fear of lack blind you to what you already have?

2. God is much more concerned about your *response* to adversity than adversity itself. Read **Philippians 4:6-8**. These verses lay out a step-by-step strategy for responding to difficult circumstances. Look at each step:

   A. *"Be anxious for nothing."* Every day of your life, you are required to interpret the events of your life and respond to them, and many of these responses are made unconsciously. The enemy is constantly lying to you about your circumstances, trying to get you to agree with his perspective. It's essential to learn how to discern when things change in your emotional, mental, and physical state and trace them back to these responses.

   B. Pray—with thanksgiving. Have you noticed that when you start telling God about your circumstances, you begin seeing them from a new perspective, even before you hear Him speak back to you? Have you noticed what happens when you begin thanking Him in the midst of difficulty? Doesn't *thanking* God for hearing you and for taking the burden of your circumstances require you to really *trust* Him to answer? How does trust in God defeat anxiety?

   C. *"...and the peace of God, which passes all understanding, will guard your hearts and minds in Christ Jesus."* The word "guard" literally means to "protect by a military force...to prevent hostile invasion." There is a place in God for you where you are protected by His peace, and you can live without struggling against the constant bombardment of the enemy's lies. Does that move you to be vigilant in bringing your life to God in prayer and thanksgiving?

   D. *"Finally, brethren...."* You have a responsibility to fill your mind with things that meet a certain criteria. Take a moment and choose one of the things in Paul's list. Make a list of synonyms for that thing—let your mind make free associations with the word. Then ask: What does this quality look like in life? Maybe you'll begin to see pictures that evoke the word, or think of memories or stories that capture that quality.

3. Another aspect of the foundation you are to have in your thinking when you face difficulty is found in the famous passage in **James 1:2-8.**

   A. In verse 4, there's a promise about *lack*. How do the previous verses say you are to respond to your circumstances in order to come into that promise? What must you believe about God and yourself if you are going to respond as you must in difficulty?

   B. Verse 5 also mentions lack. How is recognizing your lack different from building your thoughts on what you lack? How does focusing on lack end up leading you to believe that your lack is greater than God's ability to meet your needs? Why can't you receive what you need from God when you ask in doubt?

*You have probably recognized this, but faith, which is the foundation of the renewed mind, is directly opposed to fear. God is working to eliminate all fear from your life except the fear of Him. Rather than lack, your thought life must begin with faith, and another word for faith is "confidence." This word has three significant layers of meaning. The first is **boldness**, the second is **trust**, and the third is **protected communication**. God wants you to have all these things in your relationship with Him.*

Your faith enables you to step boldly into your calling, knowing that He who called you will keep you. Your faith enables you to trust God implicitly for all your needs. And your faith enables you to know that you can "confide" in God about your deepest desires and know that He hears you and will give you what you ask, as First John 5:14-15 promises.

Invite the Holy Spirit to strengthen and increase your faith in Him today in these three areas.

DAY 27

You're Prepared for the Storm

... T HAT THE MAN OF GOD MAY BE COM-
PLETE, THOROUGHLY EQUIPPED FOR
EVERY GOOD WORK.   (2 Timothy 3:18)

Most of us find ourselves in a storm and instantly conclude our job is to cry out to God to intervene and change our circumstance. But that's not the purpose of the storm; if we only cry out, we are abdicating our role in a miracle. God never allows a storm without first providing the tools to calm the storm. He wants us to use those tools to bring about a miraculous result. Think of the greatest conflict or crisis in your life in the last year. I assure you, with some examination, you can identify the tools God put in your life to take care of that problem. He allows problems into our lives so we can defeat them—not only so we can cry out to Him every time. The tools will be in the boat with us, but the enemy will fan the winds of fear to get us to forget where the tools are.

…You hear people say, "God's never early or late; He's always right on time." But God doesn't always work that way. If He always intervenes at the last minute, it's often because we didn't use the tools we'd been given in the first place.

(Quote from *The Supernatural Power of a Transformed Mind:*
Access to a Life of Miracles, Pages 102-103.)

QUESTIONS

1. Hopefully you're beginning to see that the person with a renewed mind has completely put his trust in the core truths about God's nature and in his own identity and purpose, and that this trust enables him to *respond* to the difficulties of life through faith rather than *react* in fear. Look again at the disciples' reaction to Jesus in the storm in **Mark 4:35-40.**

    A. How does the question, "Don't You care that we're perishing?" betray a lack of faith? Are the disciples convinced of Jesus' heart and nature? Why is it so essential that you understand that God is not just all-powerful, but always good and always for you in every situation?

    B. What would it have looked like for the disciples to respond with faith? What would they have said to Jesus or asked of Him?

2. In order to face difficulties with faith, you need to start with the assumption that God cares about you and has a plan to work with you to bring the solution you need. With that assumption, there are usually two things you need to do. The first thing is to pray and ask God to highlight the particular "tools" He's given you, and to give you a strategy for using them. The second thing is to *persevere*, both in getting the strategy and then in performing it. Jesus taught His disciples how to pray with perseverance in **Luke 18:1-8.** What do you make of the fact that the Lord "bears long" with you as you cry out to Him, but promises to "avenge [you] speedily"? Does God want us to persevere for His sake or for ours? Why does Jesus seem to be indicating that the faith He will look for when He returns is faith that perseveres? Are you someone who knows how to "bear long" with God, persevering in prayer?

3. When you persevere with God, He gives you so much more than a situational answer to your prayer. Look at another lesson on perseverance in **Luke 11:5-13.** Jesus draws a picture of how you must seek God with persistence for the things you need, but concludes by inferring that what we are really asking for is Him, His Holy Spirit! He Himself is the answer to everything we need. Can you see more clearly why Jesus accused His disciples of lacking faith? Their question about whether Jesus cared or not is absurd in light of the fact that He was the "exact representation" of the loving Father who was so ready to give the "good gift" of His Spirit to invade their situation. Why do you suppose God set it up so you would not be able to get what you need without getting Him? Why are you designed to need more than physical or even emotional provision? When God answers your prayers, do you feel closer to Him? Does it move you to pursue Him more?

4. Because God *is* the answer for everything you will face in life, the tools that He gives you for facing trials all have to do with releasing *Him* into your circumstances. Whether it is praise, a promise He gives you from Scripture, a prophetic word, or a testimony, it is all declaring who God is, which releases His presence and power through the word. The apostle Peter understood that what he had to release into difficult circumstances was Jesus Himself. Read **Acts 3:6-7; 4:8-10.** Do you recognize that you have Jesus? Have you experienced inviting Him into your circumstances and releasing Him through the tools He's given you?

⚔ JOURNAL / MEDITATION ⚗

Most of the tools and strategies God gives you for facing adversity are designed to get your focus (your agreement) off of the problem and onto the answer—Him. It's easy to turn a molehill into a mountain by focusing on the problem so long that it begins to be more powerful in your mind than the solution. That's when you've started believing the enemy. Jesus said that worry—which is focusing on the problem—couldn't do anything about problems, so the main thing to give yourself to is seeking the Kingdom (see Matt. 6:33). What are the tools He's given you to focus on Him? What is the revelation of His nature that He wants you to release into your present circumstances? If He's already given you a tool or strategy, ask His Spirit to strengthen you to persevere in using it today.

The Lie of the Past

...**B**UT ONE THING I DO, FORGETTING THOSE THINGS WHICH ARE BEHIND AND REACHING FORWARD TO THOSE THINGS WHICH ARE AHEAD. (Philippians 3:13b)

TODAY'S DEVOTION

Too often Christians live under the influence of yesterday's failures, blemishes, and mistakes. When we do, we depart from the normal Christian lifestyle and live under the influence of a lie. Needless to say, this lie halts the renewing of our minds and keeps us from living in the "everyday miraculous" that should be normal for every born-again believer.

...I know from personal experience that I used to willingly live under the guilt and shame of bad decisions from yesterday because I thought it helped me walk in humility. I would get down in the mouth and dwell on my shortcomings. I never was good at talking about it with friends. Instead, I internalized it. But as I focused on my character problems, they grew overwhelmingly large. I fed them with an unrenewed mind, and the power of agreement came upon the problem and multiplied its apparent size. The damage done in my own emotions and thought life was horrendous.

...People moan and groan, "I'm not worthy." Of course we're not worthy! It's time we get over it and live the Christian life anyway. Living under yesterday's condemnation doesn't make us more humble. If anything, it keeps us focused on ourselves instead of the Lord. It's much more difficult to humbly receive forgiveness we don't deserve than to walk in false humility, cloaked in yesterday's shame. When we receive free forgiveness, the one who gave it to us is honored. When He is honored, we are truly humbled.

(Quote from *The Supernatural Power of a Transformed Mind:
Access to a Life of Miracles*, Pages 106-107.)

QUESTIONS

1. Focusing on the problem instead of God's answer actually agrees with the enemy and denies the power of God, and sometimes the hardest problem to stop looking at is yourself! You know you're walking in shame and guilt instead of true conviction from the Holy Spirit by the fruit of your life. A person who has truly repented and received God's forgiveness through Jesus' blood should begin to look a lot like...well, Jesus. Read **Philippians 2:3-8**. Doesn't it boggle your mind to think that God's identity and status is less important to Him than you are? Can you see that the humility modeled by Jesus is explicitly a *self-forgetting*, a complete surrender to His Father's heart to save mankind? How does surrendering to God's heart enable you to consider others as better than yourself? Do you feel like you are seeking after more of this "mind" of Christ toward God and others?

2. The way you treat others reveals the degree to which you have received the gift of forgiveness. Jesus teaches a sobering parable on forgiveness in **Matthew 18:23-35**. Remember, this is describing the Kingdom of Heaven. God is the master and you are the one He has forgiven from the immense debt of your sin. How is it possible that you, like this servant, could be dense enough to go out and hold your brother hostage over a relatively minor grievance (which all offenses against us are considered to be by God)? Isn't it only possible because you have failed to understand the significance of your own forgiveness? Do you find it difficult to forgive people "from your heart," as the Lord requires? If so, do you also struggle to forgive yourself when you make mistakes or fail? If God has forgiven you, isn't it absurd to not forgive yourself and others?

3. The reality of being forgiven is something you need to have increasing revelation about and experience with in order to understand and live. Read **Psalm 103:2-3, 8-13**, which shows how David taught himself to meditate on God's forgiveness. David tells himself to "forget not" the Lord's benefits, among which is His forgiveness. Do you think that the human capacity to forget things is among the reasons why some end up falling into the mistake of the servant in the parable? How often do you take time to ponder what Jesus has done for you and of what you've been forgiven? Think about the fact that your sin has been removed from you "*as far as the east is from the west*." What does that mean? How completely has God taken sin away from you—from your identity and your heart?

4. Look at another parable in **Matthew 25:14-30**. This parable addresses the issue of how to truly honor God with what He has given you, and one of the primary things you've been given is *grace*—both the grace that forgives you and the grace that empowers you to live the life God has called you to; to truly become one of the "many brethren" of whom Christ is the firstborn (see Rom. 8:29). In light of the parable, consider these questions:

    A. Did the master give money to his servants simply to possess it? Likewise, does God forgive you of sin merely so you can be forgiven? For what purpose did Jesus come to free you from sin? Does it include stewing over your weaknesses and faults?

B. What did the master expect from His servants? What do you suppose it means to "invest" the grace you've been given? Wouldn't the wisest and most honorable investment be to use it towards fulfilling your calling to know God and become like Him?

C. If you receive God's grace for forgiveness but don't invest it in your calling, are you not like the servant who buried his talents in the ground? How does this parable show that the truly humble and honoring response to the gift of grace is to not merely receive it, but use it?

Take some time today to "remember the benefits" of the Lord. Tell the Lord out loud the things from which you've been forgiven, and ask Him how you can use the grace you've been given to become more like Him. The places where you've struggled the most in your life are the very areas where He wants to show Himself strong in you and make you a deliverer for others who struggle in those same areas. If He shows you anything for which you need to forgive others or for which you need to be forgiven, allow Him to lead you through that process in prayer.

Living in Our True Identity

THEREFORE, IF ANYONE IS IN CHRIST, HE IS A NEW CREATION; OLD THINGS HAVE PASSED AWAY; BEHOLD, ALL THINGS HAVE BECOME NEW. (2 Corinthians 5:17)

Whenhen we succumb to guilt and shame, we give in to the single oldest temptation in the Bible: the temptation to question our identity and God's identity.

...The Bible tells us to *"Likewise...reckon yourselves to be dead indeed to sin, but alive to God in Christ Jesus our Lord"* (Rom. 6:11). That word *reckon* means "evaluate, take an account of, do the math and come to a conclusion." We either believe that His provision was adequate or we don't.

...Remember that Jesus addressed believers as saints. We tend to think sainthood is acquitted after years of sacrificial service. Wrong. We went from rotten sinners to born-again saints in a single moment when we accepted salvation. Once the blood of Jesus has wiped out sin, you can't get any cleaner. That doesn't mean we can avoid the hurdles and issues that come with changing your life and renewing your mind. Maturity is a process. But as my associate Kris says, "You are not a sinner; you are a saint. It doesn't mean that you can't sin; it just means that you are no longer a professional."

...When the enemy brings up a sin from your past, he is talking about something non-existent. It's completely legal for you to say, "I didn't do that. That person who did that is dead. This person has never done that." Either the blood of Jesus is completely effective, or it's not effective at all.

(Quote from *The Supernatural Power of a Transformed Mind: Access to a Life of Miracles*, Pages 107-111.)

QUESTIONS

1. Since the Fall, man's view of God and himself has been distorted. One of the most basic truths about God that has been lost to mankind is that He is their Creator. Read **Isaiah 45:9-13;18-19**. If you truly believe that you were created by God, then doesn't it follow that He is really the only person who can truly give you your identity? If *He* declares that you, as a believer who has received salvation through faith in Christ, are no longer a sinner, but a saint and a son, then wouldn't clinging to the identity of a sinner be on par with telling the potter that the pot knows what it is more than its maker? According to verse 11 and 19, would you say that God wants you to hear the truth of who you are from Him?

2. Renewing the mind is the process of learning to see who you are *becoming*, because according to God, who you are becoming is who you truly are. Read **John 1:12**. Some versions say *"right to become,"* and some say *"power to become,"* because the word *exousia* includes both—it is a legal term for power of jurisdiction. Jesus' death was a legal act, as was God's adoption of those who believe on the basis of Jesus' blood sacrifice. Your identity as a saint and son is your legal standing before God. The only real question is whether you will mature into your potential as a son—whether you will fully use the power and authority you've been given to become like Jesus. Do you think focusing on who you used to be will ultimately help you become the person you have the right to be? Who should you have your eyes on in order to grow into your potential? Should there be any question in your mind that God has made all power available to you to become like Jesus?

3. Paul gives us some insights into this process of becoming in **Ephesians 4:11-24**. There are two main activities that Paul is describing.

    A. The first is the equipping and edifying of the saints through the "fivefold ministry" of apostles, prophets, evangelists, pastors, and teachers. This has to be pretty important, because the results are stunning—we'll *"grow up in all things into Him who is the head—Christ."* Can you see the language of "becoming" here? What do you suppose it means to grow up into Christ? According to verse 15, what specific activity are you to practice in order for that to occur? And according to verse 16, who *"causes the growth of the body for the edifying of itself in love"*?

    B. Christ's goal is to have it come to "the *unity* of the faith and of the knowledge of the Son of God, to a *perfect* man, to the measure of the stature of the fullness of Christ." Would you say that Christ's goal is to build ever-increasing unity, connection, interdependence, mutual submission, and accountability to His Body? How does viewing yourself and other believers as sinners oppose this purpose? Does seeing Christ's purpose for His Body shed light on His passion for you to learn how to live in forgiveness—both for yourself and others?

C. The second activity Paul describes is that of your individual responsibility to leave the "old man" and put on the "new man." These are referring to lifestyles. The link between leaving the old lifestyle and building the new is being "renewed in the spirit of your mind." Can you see that if you believe you are still the "old man," you are aligning yourself with an entire set of behaviors associated with that identity? From what you can tell, does Paul imply that this process of individually putting on the "new man"—as you agree with God's way of thinking—is the key ingredient to your participation in the larger process of the Body growing up into Christ? If so, how vital would you say it is that you learn how to live in your new identity?

*Take some time to consider the implications of this statement: "When Moses asked God, **'Who am I that I should go to Pharaoh, and that I should bring the children of Israel out of Egypt?'** (Exod. 3:11), God appeared to ignore the question by answering, **'I will certainly be with you'** (Exod. 3:12). But that was the answer! Moses said, 'Who am I?' God said, in effect, 'You are the man God goes with.' Who are you, brother or sister? You are the person that God hangs around with. You are clean and forgiven. That is your identity!"*

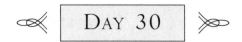

DAY 30

Learning How to Meditate

I REMEMBER THE DAYS OF OLD; I MEDITATE ON ALL YOUR WORKS; I MUSE ON THE WORK OF YOUR HANDS.   (Psalm 143:5)

⊰ TODAY'S DEVOTION ⊱

I n Eastern occult religions, meditation means emptying the mind. But biblical meditation is the opposite—it's filling the mind with God's truth.... If you've ever worried about something, you already know how to meditate! Every person, saint and sinner alike, meditates every day. The question is, what are you meditating on?

...Why does worry shout so loudly for our attention? Because if we look at it long enough, it will gain our trust. Pretty soon we begin praying out of fear, and eventually we quit praying and start looking for sympathy. We have trusted that other voice, and it won the affections of our heart.

We must get our minds set on spiritual things because as long as we fill our minds with what's happening in the natural, we restrict our effectiveness. We may rise up now and then and score a victory with the gift of faith, but we won't have the continual influence of Kingdom transformation flowing through us.

(Quote from *The Supernatural Power of a Transformed Mind:
Access to a Life of Miracles*, Pages 114-115.)

QUESTIONS

1. The word for "meditate" in Hebrew is *hagah*, which also means to "groan, growl, mutter, speak, or roar," as well as to "imagine" or "muse." Filling your mind requires the cooperation of your whole person—body, soul, and spirit. Meditation that involves speaking out loud requires that you be able to hear yourself, which requires stillness and quiet. Most people need to be in a relaxed position, and usually alone, for this listening to take place. This is also necessary for most people to be able to use their imagination for a sustained period of time. When you are moving or surrounded by a lot of activity and noise, it is very difficult to focus on anything. Do you think this kind of meditation comes easy for most of us? Do you think it is highly valued in modern culture? Would you say that this is a learned art, something that requires practice to master? Do you practice this, or do you know anyone who does? What is the fruit of embracing a consistent practice of meditation?

2. God explicitly commanded Joshua to meditate on something in particular. Read **Joshua 1:8**. The Book of the Law was the Book of Moses, which included not only the law given on Mount Sinai but Israel's entire history with God. Where was this Book to remain in Joshua? Can you see how the language connects meditation with speaking? How often was Joshua to be rehearsing out loud that which God had said and done? What is the reason given for this constant meditation? Do you think you are able to know God and observe His commands without this kind of meditation?

3. The Psalms are a wonderful tool for learning how to meditate, because most of them are David's own meditations on the nature and work of God revealed in creation and Scripture. They were specifically written to be sung or said out loud! Read **Psalm 1** aloud. What word does David use to describe the righteous man's attitude towards the law? How does this word support the idea that what we meditate on is what "wins our affections"? Did you notice that David, as did God to Joshua, declares that the fruit of this constant meditation on God's law is prosperity? Would you like for everything you do to prosper? Would you like your life to be firmly rooted, unshakable in adversity, and fruitful and wise? These are the promised results of meditation.

4. Paul instructs Timothy to meditate in **First Timothy 4:13-16**. What four things was Timothy supposed to meditate on and give himself to?

   A. The Greek word for meditate is *meletao*, which means "to care for, attend to carefully, and practice." What activities do you pursue in your life with this kind of discipline? What was the result Paul wanted from Timothy's meditation, according to verse 15? Do you recognize that the fruit of your meditation is evident to others?

   B. "Take heed to yourself" means to hold yourself to a certain focus or course. What would you say is the importance of Timothy's ability to hold himself to his practice and teaching of doctrine, considering the promised result in verse 16? Would you say that he had a *responsibility* to meditate? Would you say that you have that responsibility?

JOURNAL/MEDITATION

*Today's study is more focused on the **value** and
even the essential role of meditation in your life more than
on the details of how to meditate, and the reason is that
for much of modern society those have been profoundly lost,
mostly because distractions abound more than ever. You
are facing a difficult challenge if you set yourself to study
and practice meditation. You will not only have to go against
the grain of culture, but against your own human tendency
to be distracted and forgetful. But its significance cannot
be overstated—if you "take heed to yourself" and learn
this skill, you will not only find the "delight" that the
Psalmist talks about, but you will fulfill your call as
a disciple of Christ. In fact, it would be worth asking
if you can fulfill it without learning to meditate.*

DAY 31

Building Memorials

REMEMBER ME, MY GOD, FOR GOOD, ACCORDING TO ALL THAT I HAVE DONE FOR THIS PEOPLE. (Nehemiah 5:19)

Habakkuk 2:2 says, "*Write the vision and make it plain on tablets, that he may run who reads it.*" ...That's why I...write down God's ideas about my life whenever they are revealed to me. I mark up and underline my Bible every which way. I write down prophecies I've received on note cards and in my computer, and I carry those with me wherever I go. I post Post-It notes on the dashboard of my car. I put them all over the church sometimes so that when I walk around and pray I see cards everywhere, reminding me of what God is saying. I keep a journal for my children and my grandchildren that they might see what God did in my lifetime. We even have a staff member at our church whose entire job description is to record the miracles that happen in and through our church and with our ministry teams. I want people to know the great and mighty works of the Lord long after we're gone, so they can run with the vision even further.

...I force my imaginations to become Kingdom imaginations. The testimony of what the Lord has done helps us to remember who God is, what His covenant is like and who He intends to be in our lives. Every testimony of His work in someone's life is a prophecy for those with ears to hear. It is a promise that He'll do the same for us because *God is no respecter of persons* (see Acts 10:34) and *He is the same yesterday, today and forever* (see Heb. 13:8). But the testimony must be heard, spoken, written down, and reviewed.

...Memorial stones that we put before God—in the form of prayer and generosity—remind Him of our condition, our need and our obedience. Is it possible that God has chosen not to know certain things so that He could discover them in His relationship with us?

(Quote from *The Supernatural Power of a Transformed Mind: Access to a Life of Miracles*, Pages 115-118.)

QUESTIONS

1. There are memorials of God everywhere, but unless you know what they stand for, you won't benefit from the testimony they preserve. Today's study is going to look at some various memorials mentioned in Scripture—both memorials for us and memorials for God.

   A. God has built memorials into nature itself. Read **Genesis 8:20-22** and **9:13-16**. What natural phenomena are listed in these verses? Have you ever thought of them as reminders of God's covenant with mankind? Do you think about the fact that they remind Him as well?

   B. Read **Exodus 3:14-15**. Yahweh is the covenant name of God—the revelation that He specially gave to the children of Israel to denote Him as their God. From the beginning of history, names were much more than a way to distinguish one from the other; they signified the nature of a thing. So it is with God's name—it testifies of His nature. When you think of a person's name, don't you think of the person himself? When you think of God's name, do you think of His attributes or stories in which He played a part? Have you noticed that God gives Himself other names throughout Scripture? How many of these memorials do you know, and which ones are particularly important to your remembrance and understanding of who God is?

   C. Read **Matthew 26:6-13**. Why do you think Jesus felt that this woman's act of worship was so important to the gospel that it needed to be preached as part of it? Do you think that if her story had not been written down, it would have been preserved? Would you say that the Scriptures are the most important memorial given to mankind? Why or why not?

2. All the feasts, fasts, and sacrificial rituals that God prescribed in His covenant with Israel were memorials that kept that covenant active. Perhaps the most important of these rituals was the Day of Atonement, when the high priest would mediate for the sin of the people by bringing the blood of a lamb into the presence of God. This was the only way that a Holy God could maintain His relationship with a sinful people. However, when Christ came, He became both the lamb and the priest. Read **Hebrews 9:11-15; 10:19-22; and 12:22-24**. Hebrews 12:22-24 lists several things that exist in heaven and stand as memorials to the finished work of Christ. What are these memorials in heaven to remind us to do, according to Hebrews 10:19-22? How does it make you feel to know you have complete access to God's presence through the blood of Jesus? Which covenant does the blood of Christ remind both you and God that you have together? How is it different than the other covenant? Why does the Church no longer celebrate the rituals God prescribed in the Old Covenant?

3. One of the most important memorials the Church observes is Communion, because it reminds us of the New Covenant. Read **Luke 22:19-20**. Everything that you need to walk in the New Covenant, which is access to intimate relationship with God without the separation of sin and all that flows from that relationship (life—both now and in eternity), is provided in Christ's death. How often do you stop at this memorial and meditate on what you've received? What effects do you notice this has in your life?

⨳ JOURNAL/MEDITATION ⨳

Take Communion today and take time to tell the Lord that you are remembering what has been purchased for you. Ask the Holy Spirit to bring to mind old and new insights as you celebrate this memorial. Remind God of His promises over your life and ask Him to instruct you on how to make your own memorials in your history with Him.

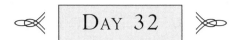
Gates of Praise

WHY ARE YOU CAST DOWN, O MY SOUL?
AND WHY ARE YOU DISQUIETED WITHIN
ME? HOPE IN GOD, FOR I SHALL YET PRAISE
HIM, THE HELP OF MY COUNTENANCE AND MY
GOD.   (Psalm 42:11)

Our troubling circumstance may last days, months, or years, instead of just an hour or two, but our approach should be the same: We must declare the goodness and faithfulness of God even in the midst of our trial, before we have an answer.

...The Bible's pairing of praise with irritation is not coincidental. When we are stuck in conflict and uncertainty, and yet we praise Him without manipulation, it is a sacrifice. It means we are reacting in a way that produces something beautiful. In that moment a gate is formed, a place of entrance where the King of glory can invade our situation.

Many people have no gates because they won't praise Him in the middle of apparent paradox.... And yet Psalm 87:2 says, *"The Lord loves the gates of Zion more than all the dwellings of Jacob."* That gate—that place of praise in the midst of conflict— is where His presence rests, where the King Himself dwells. The gate is formed when we move above human explanation and into a place of trust.

(Quote from *The Supernatural Power of a Transformed Mind: Access to a Life of Miracles*, Pages 122-123.)

QUESTIONS

1. Is your first reaction when you get a larger bill than you expected to say, "Praise You, God!"? When things don't turn out the way you hoped? When you or someone you love experiences pain or loss? When something is stolen from you? If so, then you need to share your stories of breakthrough on a regular basis! But if not, then perhaps today's study will show you the power of praise more clearly...but it will still be your job to practice using this powerful weapon God has given you. Praise is a weapon against the lies of the enemy—which is why it is so important to learn to use it in difficulty. Read **Psalm 8:2 and Matthew 21:16**. What phrase does Jesus change when He quotes the psalm? Try reading "praise" in place of "strength" in Psalm 8:2. What does praise do to the enemy? Why do you think that is?

2. Now, read **Psalm 149**. How would you describe the role of praise in spiritual warfare, according to this psalm? Keeping in mind that your battle is not against flesh and blood (see Eph. 6:12) and that your sword is the Sword of the Spirit, the Word of God (see Eph. 6:17), which is sharper than any two-edged sword (see Heb 4:12), how does your praise and declaration of the Word affect the enemy in this psalm? Look at the description of praising saints in the first 5 verses of the psalm. Do they look like grim warriors gearing up for battle? Why is rejoicing in dancing and music so powerful in the face of the enemy? Can you see that this kind of praise is not based on how you're feeling, but on faith in God?

3. In today's verse you can see that David understood that praise wasn't necessarily something that came naturally to him, but a discipline by which he called his soul into alignment with the truth. In fact, praise is exalting the name of God above your circumstances and every other force at work in your life. When you give Him that place of rule, His Kingdom (His rule and reign) is released into your life, as today's reading declares. One of the Hebrew words for praise, *yadah*, literally means to "cast down." When you praise God, you are casting down things that exalt themselves above the knowledge of God. **Psalm 9** is a wonderful guide to praise that exalts God above His enemies and yours. Read it aloud and consider the following questions.

   A. In the first two verses, David tells God four things that he *will* do. What are they, and what is the significance of the fact that these are all primarily acts of the will?

   B. Verse 1 and verse 11 connect praise with the telling of God's works. Considering that God's nature is revealed in His acts, why is rehearsing the testimony of God an essential element to the act of praise?

   C In verses 3-6 and 15-16, David tells God what He already has done, and what has happened to the wicked. How does understanding the finished work of the Cross in eternity and knowing the final judgment of the wicked give us a security and confidence in God's justice for our present circumstances? Do you feel like you have this eternal perspective when you look at current events in the world and in your personal experience?

   D. In verse 14, what is the reason David gives to God for saving him? How would you think and feel differently about your present difficulties if your primary motive or desire was a jealousy for the Lord to receive praise through them?

⨳ JOURNAL/MEDITATION ⨳

Take some time today to practice the four things that
David says He will do in Psalm 9:1-2. If you need
to go somewhere where you can be loud, then do! Consider
what it means to rejoice in God. What particular actions are
taken by someone who is rejoicing? Find out what happens
when you practice these actions, even if you don't feel like
it at first. If you truly practice praise, you will experience the
gate of heaven opening and see peace, joy, and health increase
in your life—as well as the answers to your circumstances.

DAY 33

How to Face Uncertainty

THOUGH HE SLAY ME, YET WILL I TRUST HIM. (Job 13:15)

Uncertainty causes some people to misunderstand who God is. They begin to deny God's true nature and embrace sickness and disease, poverty and mental anguish as gifts from God. That is a devastating lie from hell. It's actually blasphemy to attribute to God the work of the devil.... That's what causes people to say things like, "God gave my aunt leukemia to teach her perseverance." No way. That has never happened. If somebody's body is wracked with pain or wasting away because of disease, it's the devourer. It's not the job description of the Messiah.

...Let's get this straight: God is good all of the time. The devil is bad all of the time.... Why do disease and addiction and all the other tools of the devil continue to torment the human race? It's my conviction that if we knew more about spiritual warfare, we could thwart much of what we see. What's needed to cure the incurable and do the impossible is warfare at a level that we have never experienced.

The second thing that happens when some Christians face uncertainty is they often become intellectually offended with God.... This is intellectual offense, when you have unanswered questions that block your ability to trust in the unseen.... Questions are allowed in the Kingdom, but lack of answers must not interrupt our heart-communion with God. If we demand answers from God, we are walking in the spirit of offense.... The answer is always on the other side of our offense.

(Quote from *The Supernatural Power of a Transformed Mind:*
Access to a Life of Miracles, Pages 123-128.)

QUESTIONS

1. Job was a man who experienced incredible loss, grief, and physical pain. He was caught in the mystery of why bad things happen to good people, and he happened to be surrounded by people who had a list of reasons for him. Some told him to confess his sin, assuming that he'd done something to deserve punishment. Others told him he hadn't done something he ought to have done, and so was being punished. But eventually God cut in and pointed out that He alone had the right to tell Job the truth of his situation. Read Job 40:1-14. In uncertainty, it's easy to feel like God has some important questions to answer. But according to this passage, doesn't God's response seem to say that the issue is much more about whether we will answer His questions? What is God's primary question to Job? What is God's job description, according to verses 9-14? If you have sinned, whose job is it to tell you so? Who alone can save us in uncertainty?

2. Jesus actually promised that you would have hardship and persecution. But He also promised that you could live with the assurance that:
    - He has overcome the world (see John 16:33).
    - He is in you and He is greater than he who is in the world (see 1 John 4:4).
    - He is always with you (see Matt. 28:20).
    - He is on your side (see Rom. 8:31).
    - Nothing can separate you from His love (see Rom. 8:35).
    - He is working everything together for your good (see Rom. 8:28).
    - Every temptation you face, He faced, and He will provide you with a way of escape (see 1 Cor. 10:13).

   You can live with certainty of the nature of God and His heart toward you, no matter what the circumstances. That faith and hope are precisely what the enemy is working so hard to steal from you. Read **First Peter 1:3-9**. What is the end of your faith? Why is it important to believe that although you receive salvation at your first confession of faith, salvation is also an eternal event that you are moving towards every day of your life? If you understand that you have a lifelong journey to strengthen and guard your faith towards salvation, won't you be more aware of your need to stay on course and not give in to the enemy's lies in trials?

3. One of the biggest temptations you face is the temptation to be *disappointed.* You might think that disappointment is just a part of life, but that is a lie. Read **Proverbs 13:12** and **Romans 5:1-5**. The word "deferred" in Proverbs 13:12 literally means to be "dragged away." When something happens and you feel hopeless about a situation, it's because the enemy is trying to drag away your hope by lying to you. Everyone experiences unmet expectations in life, but where you fall into intellectual offense or redefining the nature of God is when you believe a lie in those moments of unmet expectation. If you hold on to hope, doesn't it seem to

say in Romans 5:5 that you can live without disappointment? What is the primary purpose of tribulation, according to Romans 5:3-4? Doesn't this seem to suggest that God is less interested in you experiencing difficulty than He is that you respond to difficulty with persevering faith?

4. So how do you step toward "warfare at a level that we have never experienced"? When Jesus was tempted by the devil, He was physically weak and alone in the desert. What was the weapon He chose to use? "It is written." It is vital in your relationship with God that you continue to deepen your understanding and knowledge of the Scripture. The promises of God to us in the Bible are your most reliable weapons when you are weak, tired, and hurting in times of trial. You've seen that praise is a mighty weapon in your hand. Another thing to consider today is that the prophetic words that have been spoken over your life are also weapons. Read **First Timothy 1:18-19.** How does standing behind what God has said about you keep you protected from the enemy's lies? How often do you review your prophetic words? Does hearing them again strengthen your resolve to pursue your God-given purpose, no matter what?

JOURNAL/MEDITATION

*In which areas of your life are you currently facing uncertainty or a test of some kind? What are the questions you think that God wants you to answer through this season, especially about who He is and who you are in your current circumstances? Ask the Holy Spirit to quicken your memory of the words He's spoken over your life and to show you how to stay on course in your faith. Remember the promise of Isaiah 26:3: "**You will keep him in perfect peace, whose mind is stayed on You, because he trusts in You.**"*

DAY 34

Presenting Your Body

I BESEECH YOU THEREFORE, BRETHREN, BY THE MERCIES OF GOD, THAT YOU PRESENT YOUR BODIES A LIVING SACRIFICE, HOLY, ACCEPTABLE TO GOD, WHICH IS YOUR REASONABLE SERVICE.

(Romans 12:1)

Many see the body as evil in itself, something to be ignored, pushed aside, tolerated but never really used for Kingdom purposes. But God designed the human body to be more than a tent that you dwell in. It is an instrument of God that recognizes His presence and discerns what is happening in the Kingdom realm.

...Hebrews 5:14 says a mark of maturity is having senses trained to discern good and evil. Touch, smell, sight, hearing, and taste can be trained to help us in the discernment process. Not only can we recognize the presence of God with our bodies, but those physical signs should help us discern good and evil.

...I've observed in my own body that when somebody starts talking about revival or healing, my left hand gets hot. Why, I'm not sure, but the Bible teaches that the power of God is concealed and hidden in the hands (see Hab. 3:4). When somebody talks about revival or healing, they ignite the area of the affection of my heart and the anointing is released through those affections. Paul said, "*You are not restricted by us, but you are restricted by your own affections*" (2 Cor. 6:12).

(Quote from *The Supernatural Power of a Transformed Mind:*
Access to a Life of Miracles, Pages 132, 134, 136.)

QUESTIONS

1. Jesus came in the flesh. He healed people's bodies, was resurrected with a body, and calls those who follow Him His Body. These facts alone should convince you forever that the human body is something God loves and paid a high price to redeem. The apostle Paul particularly had much to say about the value of the human body. Today, look at a number of Scriptures from his Epistles in order to gain this biblical perspective.

   A. Begin in **Romans 8:11**. What do you suppose it means that the same resurrection life given to Jesus' body lives in us and is ministering to our bodies? What value does the Holy Spirit have for our bodies?

   B. Read **First Corinthians 6:19-20**. What are the implications of the fact that you do not belong to yourself? What was the price paid for your body? How do you glorify God in your body?

   C. Read **First Thessalonians 5:23**. What does it mean that God is able to sanctify and keep your body blameless?

2. Paul's entreaty for us to offer our bodies as living sacrifices is an echo of a previous statement he makes in **Romans 6:12-13**. This is part of training your body to discern good and evil. Think about some of the members of your body for a moment. What does it mean to present your hands as instruments of righteousness? Your mouth? Your nose? Your feet? Your stomach?

3. Without your body, you cannot fulfill your God-ordained purpose on the earth. Paul likens our calling to running a race, and calls us to train our bodies for that purpose. Read **First Corinthians 9:24-27**. This last verse might initially strike you as disturbing, because Paul is literally saying that he beats himself black and blue and makes his body his own slave. But consider the rigorous physical training that Olympic athletes or Navy SEALS undergo. They don't hate their bodies; rather, they train their bodies to be instruments, which can achieve feats impossible for most of us. They are so completely focused on their task or sport that they cannot allow the appetites of their body to exercise any control over their wills and minds. What sort of physical hardships did Paul endure? What physical hardships did Jesus endure? How did these men discipline their bodies to endure so they could fulfill their purpose? What is the significance of Paul's implication that if he preaches to others without disciplining his body to run the race, he will be disqualified?

4. It is when you allow your physical appetites to rule you that the affections of your heart are drawn away from the Lord. Paul understood that in order to protect his freedom in Christ and his connection with the Holy Spirit, he had to discipline himself. Read **First Corinthians 6:12-13**. Who is the body for? Why is it important to understand the responsibility that comes with the freedom you've received in Christ? Are you aware when you allow yourself to come under the power of your appetites more than Christ? How do you discipline yourself to protect your freedom and walk toward your purpose in Christ?

JOURNAL/MEDITATION

*Jesus said that His food was to do the will of His father
(see John 4:34). As you train your body to be an instrument
of righteousness, you are training your affections to feed on
God. Today, ask the Holy Spirit to show you what your
body is for and what specific tasks you must be able
to physically perform in order to fulfill His purpose for
you. Ask Him to show you any area of change you need
to make in stewarding your body so that you can protect
your freedom and feed your affections on His will alone.*

Learning to Be a Co-Laborer

NOW IT WAS IN THE HEART OF MY FATHER DAVID TO BUILD A TEMPLE FOR THE NAME OF THE LORD GOD OF ISRAEL.   (1 Kings 8:17)

Your will is so valuable that He wouldn't violate it even at the cost of His own Son. You and I are the pearl of great price. Without an independent will, we become animated playthings, dolls, programmed toys. But with a free will, we become lovers of God and willing co-laborers with Him. And when we co-labor with Him, our ideas can literally change the course of history.

Servants aren't co-laborers; friends are. There are major differences between the mentality of each. A servant is task-oriented, wanting to know exactly what it required so he or she can do it. But a servant doesn't know the master's business from the inside.... A servant would know certain things about you.... But a servant would not share personal times with you.... God has elevated us from servant to friends. He invites us into a relationship that goes beyond employer-employee interactions. He is willing for us to engage Him...to change His mind, to direct His ideas, to share in His unfolding creative work. He doesn't lack for ideas. He just enjoys our participation.

When you become a friend of God, you don't lose the humility and obedience of a servant, but your relational perspective shifts. There is a point in our relationship with God where obedience is no longer the primary issue. That may also sound blasphemous, but it's a deep truth God wants to reveal more widely in the Church. There are levels of relationship with God that many of us have not conceived or experienced, and until we do, our co-laboring with Him will be more limited than it needs to be.

(Quote from *The Supernatural Power of a Transformed Mind: Access to a Life of Miracles*, Pages 140, 142-143.)

1. God desires a relationship with you "where obedience is no longer the primary issue" because this is what good parents desire in their relationship with their child. When the child is young, the parents must supervise the child almost constantly, feed him, clothe him, and provide for him. Gradually the child becomes capable of performing more tasks, which the parents teach him and require him to perform. The child also becomes aware of his will, and the parents must provide consequences in order to teach him which choices are healthy and which are harmful. But all along, the goal of this training is for the child to gain the wisdom, understanding, and knowledge he needs to think, act, and speak like his parents— by his own will. As an adult, the child is no longer concerned with obeying his parents so much as he is with conducting himself in the way he was taught to live in order to honor his parents and protect his relationship with them. Do you recognize the Lord drawing you into this kind of maturity?

2. The father-son relationship is exactly how God describes His relationship with man, particularly after the death of Christ. When Jesus met Mary at the tomb in John 20:17, He told her, "*Do not cling to Me, for I have not yet ascended to My Father, but go to My brethren and say to them, 'I am ascending to My father and your Father, and to My God and your God.'*" The purpose of His death was to restore our relationship with the Father. Read **Galatians 4:1-7.** Think about the differences between a slave and a son. What is the difference in their relationship with God? What is the role of free will for each of them? What are the implications of the fact that you have "the Spirit of His Son" dwelling in you? If the Spirit is what makes you recognize God as Father, then why do you suppose that many Christians are still approaching God as Master instead of Father?

3. In no other Gospel is Jesus' relationship with His Father more central than the Gospel of John. This book holds a profound revelation of the relationship you are invited to have with the Father, now that the Spirit of His Son dwells in your heart. In particular, Jesus shows what co-laboring looks like by explaining over and over that He, of His own will, was doing the will of the Father. Read **John 10:15-18.** How would you describe Jesus' relationship with His Father in these verses? Is He robotically obeying His Father? What kind of love do you see between the Father and the Son? Can you really be a co-laborer unless you have a love for Him that leads you to lay down your life and will for His will?

4. The enemy knows that if you begin to enter into that deep, sacrificial love relationship with the Father and set your heart to only do and say what He is saying and doing, as Jesus did, you too will begin to destroy his works. He is hard at work doing everything he can to hinder your friendship with God by stealing your freedom. You lose your freedom when you begin using it for something other than loving God and loving others. Read **Galatians 5:13-18, 22-23.** Why does using your freedom for anything but relationship end up leading you back into bondage? You know you are growing in freedom by the increasing presence of the fruit of the Spirit in your life. Do those fruits describe the quality of your relationship with God and others? Which qualities are strong, and which qualities do you particularly want to see more of in your life?

*The relationship of a co-laborer is the relationship Jesus described in John 14:4-5: "**Abide in Me, and I in you. As the branch cannot bear fruit of itself, unless it abides in the vine, neither can you, unless you abide in Me. I am the vine, you are the branches. He who abides in Me, and I in him, bears much fruit; for without Me you can do nothing.**" Learning to abide in Christ and the Father is the primary task of freedom, because all fruitfulness flows from intimacy. Today, spend some time asking the Holy Spirit what it means to abide in Christ.*

He Wants to Give You Your Desires

H E WILL FULFILL THE DESIRE OF THOSE WHO FEAR HIM. (Psalm 145:19)

God is enamored of your desires. He wants to see what makes you tick. Yes, He made you and knows everything about you, but He can only commune with you as you open yourself up in relationship with Him.

...When we commune with the Father, our desires are pure. Remember that Jesus said, *"Whatever things you ask when you pray, believe that you receive them, and you will have them"* (Mark 11:24). What do you desire when you are praying? What do you desire in that place of communion with the Lord? ...We don't dream independent of God, but because of Him.

...God trusts the heart of a man who is lost in friendship with Him. As we come into intimacy with Him, more of what takes place is a result of our desires, not only of our receiving specific commands from heaven.... As He sees you and me surrender to His agenda, He's suddenly interested in hearing what we have to say. Our yieldedness and surrender make Him vulnerable to our dreams.

...Your desires, far from being evil, are intended to make you strong and healthy in all areas of life. The Bible calls the fulfillment of your desires a tree of life (Proverb 13:12; 13:19).... Desire is part of God's system, His economy. He draws us into intimate friendship with Him, then responds to our desires and prayers, and answers them. When He does, it releases the courage of eternity into us. When our desires go unfulfilled, our bodies and spirits suffer together. One of the causes of sickness and disease is disappointment that is never dealt with redemptively.

(Quote from *The Supernatural Power of a Transformed Mind: Access to a Life of Miracles*, Pages 144-146, 151-152.)

QUESTIONS

1. God's goal has never been for you merely to obey Him. He gave you a free will so you could obey Him out of love. Similarly, God's goal for His relationship with you has never been for it to primarily focus on meeting your needs, but on awakening your desires. God doesn't need anything, so a relationship with Him based on needs is completely one-sided, and in fact, is no relationship at all. God didn't save you to meet your needs; He saved you because He loved you (see John 3:16). God truly wants a loving, intimate relationship with His people. For this reason, God not only calls His relationship with you that of Father and son, but of husband and wife. Read **Ephesians 5:22-31**. What is the sign of Christ's love for the Church, according to verse 25? Why does He want you to be "holy and without blemish"? Can you be united to Him if you are not made holy as He is holy? How does Christ consider His relationship with the Church, and therefore, what does He do for her, according to verse 29? Would you say that what is true for Christ is also true for you, that if you love Him, you love yourself also, because you are one flesh with Him? In this kind of relationship, what is the primary desire of each person?

2. It is when you understand God's longing to have this intimate relationship with you that His interest in your desires makes sense. But in that relationship, *your* focus is on what *He* desires. Read **Psalm 37:3-5**. How would you read these verses if your perspective was as someone whose main goal was to find out what God desires and do what you can to fulfill those desires? Why does God desire you to trust Him? Why does God desire you to do good? Why does God desire you to dwell in "the land"—the place of His protection, care, provision, and promise? Why does God desire you to feed on His faithfulness? Why does God desire for you to delight in Him? Would you say that these are the demands of a righteous God or the desires a loving husband has for his wife?

3. Because God's goal is relationship, His primary goal in your conversations with Him (prayer) is not to have you report what you need and then work it out for you. His primary goal is for you to experience the "tree of life" that results when your desires are fulfilled. What does that tree of life produce in you? Read **John 16:23-24**. Why does God want you to receive what you ask for? Why does answered prayer produce that in you? How does it affect your connection with God? Now read **Proverbs 17:22** and **Nehemiah 8:10b**. What does joy produce in your body and life?

4. The desires that God is interested in are the desires of your *heart*. Your heart is much more than your emotions. In Scripture, your heart includes your soul, your will, your mind, your thinking, knowledge, reflection and memory, your conscience, and the seat of your appetites, emotions, passions, and courage. It is the very center and power of your being. Read **Proverbs 4:23**. What springs out of your heart? Can you see why the heartsickness that comes from disappointment (see Prov. 13:12) affects your whole life? How do you think it will affect your life if the dreams and desires God longs to awaken in your heart are never born through intimacy with Him?

JOURNAL/MEDITATION

*The words "delight" and "desire" are closely related in
Hebrew. If you were to substitute the word "desire" for
"delight" in Psalm 37:4, it would say, "Desire the Lord,
and He will give you the desires of your heart." That
would mean that He would give you Himself! What
could be better than for God to demonstrate the fact that
He is the answer and fulfillment of every desire and dream
of your heart? The relationship God invites you into is a
relationship of incredible richness and joy, beyond anything
you've ever imagined. It is eternal life. Take some time
today to thank the Lord for His incredible love and ask
Him to continue to draw you into the fullness of joy He
designed for you to experience in your relationship with Him.*

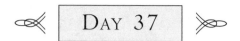

Releasing Creativity

A ND I HAVE FILLED HIM WITH THE SPIRIT OF
GOD, IN WISDOM, IN UNDERSTANDING, IN
KNOWLEDGE, AND IN ALL MANNER OF WORK-
MANSHIP.   (Exodus 31:3)

Dreaming with God unlocks deep reservoirs of creativity in each and every person, in different areas of gifting and talent. But in too many sectors of the Church, creativity is on lockdown because people fear their desires and dreams. Religion, cruel and boring, bottles up the creative impulse God has put inside of every person. Each of us has a right and responsibility to express ourselves creatively in whatever area of life that interests us. Yet so many of us have the horrible habit of doing things the way they have always been done, for reasons of fear and safety....

Many Christians pray, and when their mind wanders they think it's the devil distracting them. That may sometimes be the case, but maybe our "devil" is too active and our God too inactive. When your mind wanders, maybe God is leading you to creative solutions to problems.

...Philippians 4:19...says *"according to His riches in glory by Christ Jesus."* A Jewish rabbi was asked about that phrase and he said, "It means God, out of His realm of glory and dominion, will release to His people ideas, concepts, creative things, and witty inventions that will cause tremendous provision to come to them."

Pay attention to Kingdom imaginations. I don't mean the thundering voice in the sky, but the fresh ideas that gallop through your head throughout the day....You see, the Church won't transform cities through continuous revival meetings but by allowing Kingdom creativity and power to flow into communities.

(Quote from *The Supernatural Power of a Transformed Mind:
Access to a Life of Miracles*, Pages 147, 149-150.)

QUESTIONS

1. Perhaps the strongest reason for arguing that Christians should be the most creative people on the planet is the fact that they have the Spirit of God dwelling inside them, and creating is what He does best. Take a look at the Spirit's creative activities in Scripture, starting in **Genesis 1:1-2** and **Proverbs 8:22-31**. How does the Holy Spirit/Wisdom describe His/Her role beside the Lord in Proverbs 8:30? What is the significance of the fact that the Spirit who designed the entire universe lives inside of you? What particular emotions does He express in verses 30-31? Do you think the fact that God created you in His image with a creative capacity is one of the reasons why the Spirit particularly delights in the sons of men?

2. Often the word "inspired" is used to describe a person's creative expression. The word literally means "moved by the Spirit"—just as He "moved" over the face of the waters in Genesis. One of the prime examples of this kind of inspiration in the Old Testament is in **Exodus 31:1-6**. In what four areas of the Spirit were these men filled? Why are these qualities necessary for creativity? Would you say that the way to step into greater creativity is to pursue greater revelation?

3. Why do you think religion shuts down creativity? The reasons are manifold, but consider the following statements: Religion is based on the belief that you are fundamentally a sinner who must be controlled by rules. It controls by fear and intimidation, which are the enemies of love. It demands that you focus on doing what's right and not doing what's wrong, that you not think and that you not ask questions. Its goal is to appease God rather than know Him. It values going through the motions more than sincerity of heart. It values being right more than being loving. It certainly has no sense of humor. It is tyrannical, working to rob the very thing Jesus died to give back to you: your free will, by which you can enter into a free and loving relationship with your Father. Has this been your experience of religion? Can you see how religion is fundamentally opposed to a relationship with the Creator marked by the curiosity, joy, diversity, pleasure, and freedom that encourage creativity?

4. God created with His Word, and He tells us that life and death are in the power of your tongue as well (see Prov. 18:21). Look at **Romans 4:17b** and **First Corinthians 14:1-4**. Have you ever noticed that some people have a knack to see potential or possibilities wherever they are? They look at an empty field and see a beautiful park or a community center. They look at the structure of a molecule and go, "I wonder what this would do if I combined it with this element?" This is the creative nature of the God who calls things that are not as though they are. The gift of prophecy has the same creative role. Prophecy edifies, and the word "edify" means to erect a building. Doesn't that sound like the "master craftsman" Holy Spirit at work? Does this explain why Paul tells us to "earnestly pursue" prophecy? Have you ever thought of prophecy as a creative gift? Do you think that the daydreams that "gallop through your head" could be ideas that God wants you to prophesy into being?

JOURNAL / MEDITATION

*Are there any particular areas of your life where you
need a creative solution to a problem, or is there an area
of society or the world that you have a desire to see change?
Take some time today to invite the Holy Spirit to take you
on a journey in your imagination to a place where you can
see what the change would look like in detail. Then ask
Him to lead you into prophetic revelation and insight as to
how that change could happen. Then let Him guide you into
prophetic declaration, calling that which is not into being.*

What Is Spiritual Inheritance?

T HE SECRET THINGS BELONG TO THE LORD OUR GOD, BUT THOSE THINGS WHICH ARE REVEALED BELONG TO US AND TO OUR CHILDREN FOREVER, THAT WE MAY DO ALL THE WORDS OF THIS LAW.   (Deuteronomy 29:29)

It's a biblical concept that one generation would provide a boost for the next. A spiritual inheritance works the same way.

...A spiritual inheritance is about making us more effective and efficient in our representation of the King and His Kingdom. It is not for our gratification. It's delightful, it's enjoyable, it's pleasant, it's encouraging, but it's not simply for personal consumption. It is to open doors so that the King and His Kingdom have influence in more places than before.

A spiritual inheritance differs from a natural inheritance in one key way: A natural inheritance gives us something we did not have before. But a spiritual inheritance pulls back the curtain and reveals what we already have permission to possess.

...When we learn of our inheritance, suddenly we have "spending power" with God. We call on resources we didn't know about before. When a previous generation passes on a spiritual inheritance, they pass on all the knowledge and experience they gained in a certain spiritual area.

...Proverbs 13:22 says, *"A good man leaves an inheritance for his children's children."* Righteousness causes us to realize that our daily decisions affect several generations away. We must learn to sow into the welfare of a generation we may never live to see.

(Quote from *The Supernatural Power of a Transformed Mind: Access to a Life of Miracles*, Pages 154-155, 166.)

QUESTIONS

1. Jesus' plan for spreading the revelation of the Kingdom throughout the earth was to entrust that revelation to a small group of disciples who would teach and train their converts both to observe Christ's commands and to pass them on to their own converts. Jesus' plan was generational, because that is the nature of God revealed throughout Scripture.

   A. Look at the progression of this revelation beginning in **Genesis 1:27-28**. If God told Adam and Eve to fill and subdue the earth, what does that imply about the state the earth was in at that point? Why do you think God wanted the earth filled with people?

   B. After Adam and Eve sinned, God began to make covenants with man. Look at the first one in **Genesis 9:8-11**. Who was included in this covenant, even though they were not yet present?

   C. The next one is in **Genesis 17:1-9**. What is the first promise God gives to Abraham in verse 2? How does this echo what He said to Adam? How many times does God mention Abraham's descendants?

   D. Look at how God kept His covenant with Abraham in the life of his grandson, Jacob. Read **Genesis 35:9-12**. Which phrases are direct echoes of God's words to Adam and Abraham?

   E. Four hundred years later, God remembers His covenant with Abraham, Isaac, and Jacob and leads the people of Israel into the desert, where He makes a covenant with them. Read **Exodus 19:3-6**. Considering the progression you've seen so far, why does God want a "holy nation" of His own on the earth?

2. Israel failed to keep their covenant with God and generation after generation missed out on the benefits God wanted to give them. The problem was sin, and so God sent His Son to deal with the problem and establish the New Covenant with those who would come into relationship with Him through Jesus' blood. But God's plan to fill the earth and subdue it through His sons endures in the New Covenant. Read **First Peter 2:9-10**. Can you see that God's plan to have a holy nation has never changed? Does this support the fact that He is still planning to establish His kingdom through a covenant that extends through the generations?

3. Understanding the nature of God and His plan for advancing His Kingdom is vital for understanding your calling and identity. As today's reading reminds you, the righteousness that you obtain through faith in Christ is meant to renew your minds to think in terms of generations—both to receive the wealth of previous generations and to leave an inheritance to those whom you will raise up after you. The first step in accessing your inheritance is firmly establishing in your minds and hearts that you are a legitimate son or daughter of God, because it is that

identity which entitles you to the mysteries of the Kingdom. Review **Romans 8:14-17**. What qualifies you as a son of God, according to verse 14? Who are you heirs of, according to verse 17?

4. Perhaps the most vital revelation each believer needs to have is a revelation of covenant. God has revealed Himself as a God of covenant relationship, and this is the type of relationship that He calls you to have with Himself and with others. The purpose of this is that covenant affects generations. God expresses His anger at broken covenants because of how they affect the future. Read **Malachi 2:13-15**. Remember, marriage is the covenant between people that most resembles the relationship of Christ and the Church. What is it that God seeks from this covenant, according to verse 15? Why is it important that both your spiritual children and your natural children are born into this kind of covenant?

*As an heir of God, you inherit everything that belongs
to Him as well as the revelation of who He is through
relationship with Him. Ephesians 1:13-14 explains that
you have already received the Holy Spirit Himself as the
down payment of that inheritance, and His job is to reveal
to you what else is yours by inheritance. That revelation
is so vast that no one person can possibly perceive it
or make use of it. This is one reason why God desires
to have a holy nation of sons who can all carry a different
part of that revelation and "put the will of God on display."
While it may be true that past generations of believers
have dropped the ball in raising up the next generation
to use their inheritance, God still has that inheritance
in His keeping and still plans to bestow it on His Church
in order to equip her to fulfill every purpose and plan He
has prepared to make her "**a praise in the earth**" (Isa. 62:7).*

*In your prayer time, ask the Holy Spirit to not only
begin giving you keys for accessing your inheritance,
but keys for understanding the purpose of that
inheritance, especially as it pertains to investing
in and raising up the next generation to walk in it.*

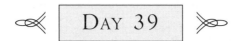

Occupy and Advance

FOR TO EVERYONE WHO HAS, MORE WILL BE GIVEN, AND HE WILL HAVE ABUNDANCE; BUT FROM HIM WHO DOES NOT HAVE, EVEN WHAT HE HAS WILL BE TAKEN AWAY. (Matthew 25:29)

The quickest way to lose something is to take a defensive posture where we maintain what we have instead of working to increase it.... When a person gets set free, there is a moment when he is absolutely clean and purged from filthiness. From that moment on he has the responsibility of managing that liberty.

...When the victories of past generations go unoccupied, they become the platform from which the enemy mocks the victories of the past generation. Worse yet, that unoccupied territory becomes the military encampment from which the enemy launches an assault against the people of God to erase from their memories their inherited victories.

...Every generation of revivalists has been fatherless as it pertains to the move of the Spirit. Every generation has had to learn from scratch how to recognize the Presence, how to move with Him, how to pay a price. The answer to this tragedy is inheritance, where you and I receive something for free. What we do with it determines what happens in the following generations. God is serious about returning for a glorious Church. He's serious that nations should serve Him—not just a token representation from every tribe and tongue—but entire nations, entire people groups apprehended by God Himself.

(Quote from *The Supernatural Power of a Transformed Mind:*
Access to a Life of Miracles, Pages 157-161.)

QUESTIONS

1. If there is one word to describe the revelation of God's nature that you inherit from past generations, it is the word *testimony*. Read **Hebrews 11:1-2;39-40**. What did the heroes of faith gain from their lives of faith? What are they waiting for now?

2. Now read **Hebrews 12:1-2** and **Revelation 1:5a**. A witness is someone who gives a testimony. You are surrounded by the testimonies of those who proved the will of God on earth through faith, and they are watching to see how you will choose to learn from their legacy. Not only that, you have the testimony of Jesus Himself. He has "finished the race" set before you. What was the joy set before Jesus? Could you say that this "race set before you" is also the "responsibility of managing that liberty" Jesus has purchased for you? How does this picture of a life of forward motion—in the sight of those who have gone before us—correspond with the idea that you were entrusted with the grace of salvation in order to advance the Kingdom for the next generation? Can you see that the generations before us and the generations after us are each strongly affected by the choices of each?

3. Now go on to **Hebrews 12:14-17**. What did Esau fail to value? Why is this such a serious offense, in light of your birthright in Christ and that which you are meant to inherit? Have you known people who have come to Christ but failed to value their birthright and "sold it," if you will, for something as petty as a bowl of soup? How do you suppose the Body of Christ can "look carefully" in order to keep people from committing this offense?

4. As you just saw in Hebrews 12:1, the only way to use your inheritance of testimony from the previous generations is to use those testimonies as *weapons* in the process of laying aside the weights and besetting sins, and as *fuel* for running the race. You also want to "obtain a good testimony." As long as the Body of Christ is still in the process of becoming the "glorious Church," the life of every Christian will be in motion towards that. The idea that you can get "fire insurance" from Christ and just coast through life on earth should be considered in light of **First Corinthians 3:9-15**. Now, this passage is a word primarily to those who are called to build the church—the gifts of Christ mentioned in Ephesians 4:11. But each believer has a responsibility for their influence over the next generation of believers, especially their children, both natural and spiritual. If you follow the metaphor Paul is building in the passage, it would seem that God holds you accountable for how you build the next generation. If they endure (obtain eternal life), then you receive your reward, but if they "burn," you will be saved, "yet so as through fire." This is sobering, but worth considering in light of the fact that the enemy is working to reclaim the territory that was stolen from him when you became Christ's. He wants you and your future generations as surely as God does. What do you suppose the "gold, silver, and precious stones"—the most enduring materials in Paul's list—represent? What is the significance of the fact that these

are also the costliest materials? What sort of materials should you be using to build the next generation?

5. The testimony of Scripture indicates that it is not only possible to build the next generation to endure in their faith, but that a person can enter into such a place of favor with God that He blesses many of your generations to come. Like Abraham, David stepped into this place of favor. Read **Second Samuel 7:12-16** and **Isaiah 9:6-7**. Who reigns on the throne of David? Is it possible that if you seek to become a man or woman "after God's heart" that you could be part of the establishing of the increase of Jesus' government on the earth?

*If you keep your eyes fixed on Jesus and keep running toward Him, persevering through trials and shaking off every burden and sin that would distract you, you **will** obtain a good testimony. Peter says that your faith is more costly than gold (see 1 Pet. 1:7), so you will also obtain the costliest material with which to lay the foundation for the next generation. Today, ask the Holy Spirit to strengthen your gaze on Jesus. Meditate on Him, and ask Him, the "faithful witness," to reveal a greater measure of both what you have received through His death and what He wants you to give to those that will come after you. Remember, His Word comes fully equipped to perform itself.*

Inheritance Makes a Greater Anointing Available

BEHOLD, I SAY TO YOU, LIFT UP YOUR EYES AND LOOK AT THE FIELDS, FOR THEY ARE ALREADY WHITE FOR HARVEST.   (John 4:35)

Inheritance helps us to build truth on top of truth....Truth is progressive and multi-dimensional.... There are measures and levels of anointing that cause the reality of the Scripture to change for us. In fact, a generation is now forming, I pray and believe, that will walk in an anointing that has never been known by mankind before, including the disciples. This generation won't need natural illustrations to help them understand what their spiritual task is. They will move into spiritual territory that defies the natural order.

...Jesus walked in such an anointing, carrying the Spirit without measure, which instantly defied the natural principles that illustrated spiritual truths. The more you and I become empowered and directed by the Spirit of God, the more our lives should defy the natural principles that release spiritual realities.

...We must lift our eyes to see from His perspective. A greater vision/revelation makes a greater anointing available, if I'll *earnestly pursue spiritual gifts.*

...Before Jesus returns there will be the community of the redeemed walking under the influence of their inheritance, *a city whose builder and maker is God.* There will be a generation that steps into the cumulative revelation of the whole Gospel. There will be a generation that lifts their eyes and sees that supernatural season in which every single person is harvestable now, and have the anointing necessary to carry it out.

(Quote from *The Supernatural Power of a Transformed Mind:*
Access to a Life of Miracles, Pages 162-165, 167.)

QUESTIONS

1. Jesus clearly intends for His Kingdom to be established through the increasing presence and activity of His Holy Spirit resting on His growing Body. Look again at His promise in John 14:12 and John 16:7. Why do you think Jesus promised that those who believe in Him would do greater works? What event occurred because Jesus returned to the Father? Who is the Helper, and why does He enable you to do greater works?

2. Remember, from the beginning God has made His plan to fill the earth with His glory contingent on the multiplication of His people. The Holy Spirit's coming to dwell in the life of a believer is what makes the multiplication of Christ—the new Adam—possible. God *will* establish His Kingdom on earth as it is in Heaven through the co-laboring of His Spirit and His Church. But you have this privilege and responsibility to "earnestly pursue spiritual gifts." Take a look at the passages on spiritual gifts in First Corinthians 12:7-11; 14:1-4; and 14:24-25. The word for "desire" in First Corinthians 14:1, literally means "to burn with zeal." This is no passive inclination you are to have for spiritual gifts; it is an all-consuming passion. But why do you think prophecy is the gift you are to pursue the most? What is the result "if all prophesy"? Why is this so important? Considering that there is an anointing which makes everyone "harvestable" now, what role do you think prophecy is meant to play in light of this result?

3. Now look at Acts 2:1-21. What did the men of Jerusalem hear the disciples speaking about in verse 11? What are the particular signs of the outpouring of the Spirit in verses 17 and 18? Why do you think these revelatory manifestations are so important? What is the final result of this outpouring in verse 21? Considering Paul's word about the effects of prophecy in First Corinthians, would it be fair to draw a correlation here between the outpouring of the Spirit, prophecy, and the harvest?

4. The whole process of renewing your mind is the process of lifting your eyes to see from His perspective. This process occurs entirely through your relationship with the Holy Spirit. Look at John 16:8-15. Remember what will happen to the unbeliever when he comes among the prophesying Church in First Corinthians 14? According to this verse, who does the work of conviction? Does this imply that the Holy Spirit Himself is released to work when you prophesy? What does this passage reveal about the process by which you receive prophetic revelation? When the Holy Spirit shows you something that is coming, what should your response be?

5. Read John 17:18-21. Who will believe in Christ if the Church is in complete unity with God? Would you say that this verse implies that your unity with God and with other believers is the first thing, and that the harvest is a matter of course if that unity is established? Do you think if Jesus prayed to the Father to make us one, anything can keep it from happening? What sort of things do you think the Lord could invite you to do, pray, and declare in order to agree with Christ's prayer in your relationship with the Holy Spirit and with the Body of Christ?

*The anointing that is available to you is not
an impersonal, spiritual power. The anointing is the
Holy Spirit. Jesus was called the "Christ" not because
He did miracles, but because of the One who rested upon
Him. If you are going to pursue a deeper anointing to see
the Kingdom break through in the way that you have
dreamed and in ways you haven't yet dreamed, it will
only take place as you seek the Holy Spirit as the first
person in everything. His voice, His perspective, and His
heart must be the most powerful motivators in your life. Seek
Him, worship Him, and give your heart today to Him afresh.
He will accomplish all He has begun to do in your life!*

Additional copies of this book and other
book titles from DESTINY IMAGE are
available at your local bookstore.

For a complete list of our titles,
visit us at www.destinyimage.com
Send a request for a catalog to:

Destiny Image® Publishers, Inc.
P.O. Box 310
Shippensburg, PA 17257-0310

*"Speaking to the Purposes of God for this
Generation and for the Generations to Come."*